Have a Chat
with a Biblical Woman

By
Jacquelyn Griggs

Dedication

Dedicated to my granddaughters Sarah, Katie,
and Jessica

With special recognition to my husband, Donnie,
whose love, strength, and encouragement made this
book possible.

Foreword

───⟨⟩⟨⟩───

Have you ever wondered what it would be like to sit down and have a chat with a lady from the Bible? Wouldn't it be nice to see if she had some of the same struggles that you and I experience and see how she handled them? *Have a Chat* is just that book. Travel with me back in time and meet thirty-one women who God chose to memorialize in His Word. Create a time to listen and understand what these ladies were thinking and feeling. My prayer is that you will let them speak to you. Find out why God chose these women to play a part in history and let them encourage you to continue on in your daily walk with the Lord. Each lady is an actual biblical person. Each story is written in first person just as if she walked out of the Bible to tell her story. The Scripture is given where the lady is mentioned. The story is a fictional account of what may have happened. It describes how she might have felt and thought through her life here on earth. Read a chapter a day and then think or meditate on why God chose to tell that particular story. Try to learn the spiritual lessons from each lady. These ladies have much to teach us.

Table of Contents

_ᏮᏮ_

"A Thirsty Woman"

It seems just like any other day, doesn't it? But what if today you were to meet Jesus face to face in a conversation? What would He have to say to you? Would this conversation be life-changing? Listen and hear a story from a lady who had a face to face conversation with Jesus.

It is a hot, dry day and my water pot is empty. I need water, but I am not going with the other ladies at the end of the day. It will be cooler, but I don't want to put up with their rebuking looks and remarks. I don't get along well with them. I have a slight problem with relationships. Anyway, I decide to go to Jacob's well at noon this day. It is very hot, but I know I'll be the only one there. Well, you can imagine my amazement when I see someone sitting by the well. And another amazing thing is that He is a Jew. Jews never come this way.

"What is He doing here?" I wonder.

Then He speaks to me. Now, wait a moment here! First, here is a Jew at the well, and next, He speaks to me. He asks me to draw him some water. So I say to Him, "How is it that You, being a Jew, ask me for a drink since I am a Samaritan woman?" I give Him some water, and I just want to get my water and go. But He says something really strange. He says something about giving me "living water." What is He talking about?

I say, "You don't have anything to draw with. How can you give me this water?"

Now this conversation gets really weird. He says He will give me water and I will never thirst again. So I think, "Yeah! That will be great; no more going to the well. Think of the time that will save."

I say, "Give me some of that water!"

You'll never believe what He says next. He says, "Go get your husband." Now where did that come from? I thought we were talking about water; now He wants to see my husband? I think I'll trick Him, so I tell Him I don't have a husband.

He says, "You have rightly said, for you have had five husbands, and the one you are with is not your husband."

Well, I told you at the beginning I have a problem with relationships. But how does He know that?

I say, "You must be a prophet." I want to get Him off this topic, so I decide to impress Him with my religious knowledge. This conversation just keeps getting stranger and stranger. I'll relay what happens next.

I say, "Sir, I perceive that You are a prophet. Our fathers worshiped in this mountain, and Your people say the place where we must worship is in Jerusalem."

He tells me, "Woman, believe Me, an hour is coming when you will worship the Father neither on this mountain or in Jerusalem. You worship what you do not know; we worship what we know, for salvation is from the Jews. But an hour is coming, and now is, when the true worshipers will worship the Father in spirit and truth; for they are the kind of worshipers the Father seeks. God is spirit, and those who worship Him must worship in spirit and in truth."

I am getting confused, so I tell Him I knew the Messiah was coming and would tell us the truth. You can imagine my amazement when He says, "I am He!" The light finally comes on! I am talking with the Messiah—the Savior of the world!

The disciples are coming back from the city, but I am so excited I leave my water pot and run to tell the people in Samaria what I have experienced. I tell them this man told me about everything I had done and He is surely the Messiah. The people come out to meet Jesus the Messiah and He stays two days with us. Here I started the day out so worried about everyday things, and then I meet the Messiah. Oh, how He changed my life! I don't have to seek love in all the wrong ways anymore. I put my love and trust in the man who knows all things about me. Whenever I go to the well, I remember my encounter with my Messiah.

"Blessed are those who hunger and thirst for righteousness for they will be filled" (Matthew 5:6). Have you had an encounter with Jesus? He knows all about you and loves you anyway. He is waiting for you.

Our fathers worshiped in this mountain, and you people say that in Jerusalem is the place where men ought to worship. Jesus said to her, "Woman, believe Me, an hour is coming when neither in this mountain nor in Jerusalem will you worship the Father. You worship what we know, for salvation is from the Jews. But an hour is coming, and now is, when the true worshipers will worship the Father in spirit and truth; for such people the Father seeks to be His worshipers. God is spirit, and those who worship Him must worship in spirit and truth."

John 4:20-24

Verses of the Day: Psalm 9:9-10

The Lord also will be a stronghold for the oppressed,
A stronghold in times of trouble,
And those who know Thy name will put their trust in
  Thee;
For Thou, O Lord, hast not forsaken those who seek
  Thee.

"A Devoted Woman"

W ould you like to meet the first woman to hold baby Jesus besides Mary? Today we go to the temple in Jerusalem about forty days after the birth of Jesus. Here is the Prophetess Anna to tell her story.

I remember listening to my father, Phanuel, talk about our God. The stories about our nation's history were always fascinating to me. Our family was from the Tribe of Asher which was descended from the eighth son of Jacob. I had a firm foundation in our belief and in how we should honor God. My father was close to God. His name meant "the face of God." He taught us to seek God for His direction in everything we did. I trusted my father when he chose a husband for me. I knew he would be one who was like my father and loved God. I was so excited for my wedding day to come. My name is Anna, and my father used to call me his "little grace." I could see he was excited for me as well. I thought my life was complete.

We lived in the city of Jerusalem. After several years of marriage, I was concerned because we didn't have any children. But my father and husband told me to be patient and wait on the Lord. We lived close to the temple, and each day I would go and pray. I would pray for God's will to be done and for me to accept whatever the decision was going to be. My husband and I became close to the Lord and close to each other during this time. We were learning to depend on God for our joy and contentment in life.

Then one day my father came to the house and told me my husband had died. I couldn't believe it. We had been married just seven years. My father hugged me and cried with me, but he told me I must look to the Lord for my strength. I didn't know what I was going to do. How was I going to live? I soon learned my help would come from the Lord. My husband and I had attended the temple on a regular basis. We enjoyed just going to the temple to pray together. I went to the temple to pray and seek direction from God. The priests there knew me and my circumstances. They said I could help around the temple even though I was not from the Tribe of Levi; I was from the Tribe of Asher, if you remember. But *Asher* means "blessed," and at that time I felt so blessed. Even in my distress, I could see the hand of God.

I lived close to the temple so I could be there every day. I would spend time in prayer and fasting. I could hear the reading of the scrolls. I learned much. I especially enjoyed the readings about the coming Messiah. Simeon, a priest at the temple, would speak much about this great Redeemer for our nation. I would ask him questions and say, "Where?! When!?" Simeon would tell me to be patient and pray and trust God because His timing is always perfect.

One day Simeon came and told me the Lord had revealed to him he would not die before he was able to see the Messiah. Now I thought, "Great! Any day now we will see the Messiah." I would go to the temple each day with great anticipation. This went on for many years. And I mean many years! I had been married seven years when my husband died. Now I had been working in the temple for eighty-four years. So I was getting up there in years. Simeon kept saying to have faith and keep praying.

One day I went to the temple as usual. I saw a young couple with their baby talking with Simeon. How wonderful to see a young couple bring their son to be dedicated to the Lord. But then I heard Simeon speak and say he could now go home to be with God because he had seen the "salvation of the nation." It was "He." I mean it was the Messiah! I ran to the couple and looked upon the babe. The Lord spoke to my heart. Here was the redemption of Israel, the long-awaited Messiah. I laughed. I cried. I hugged Mary and Joseph. I was so excited. Our God was faithful and had not forgotten His people. I held the baby Jesus in my arms. My old arms trembled as I realized who I held. Can you imagine my joy?! I couldn't wait to tell everyone I met how the redemption of Israel was at hand.

I can tell you there were days during those eighty-four years that it was difficult to remain faithful and keep trusting. But God was in control at all times. I just had to remember His faithfulness and His goodness to me, and He renewed my strength. I simply claimed His promises and He fulfilled them. As you continue your walk in this world, remember this great truth! Our God always fulfills His promises.

And then as a widow to the age of eighty-four. She never left the temple, serving night and day with fasting and prayers. At that very moment she came up and began giving thanks to God, and continued to speak of Him to all those who were looking for the redemption of Jerusalem.

Luke 2:37 and 38

Verse of the Day: Psalm 31:24

Be strong and let your heart take courage,
All you who hope in the Lord.

"A Courageous Woman"

W ouldn't you think a princess would have everything
she wanted and nothing to worry about? Let me
introduce to you Jehosheba. Her father was King Joram, so
she grew up in a palace and had everything at her command,
but she still wasn't satisfied. Here she is to tell her story.

Yes, I am a princess. If you go back into my ancestry,
you'll find my grandparents were King Ahab and Queen
Jezebel. You may have heard about them. My father is King
Joram, King of Judah. He had many wives, but his main wife
is Queen Athaliah. She's the daughter of King Ahab and
Queen Jezebel. She's also my stepmother. You talk about a
wicked stepmother! She was it! She was only interested in
worshipping Baal and gathering more and more riches. I had
everything riches could buy, and my brother Ahaziah and
I were taught to serve Baal and seek only our own desires.
Yet in that great big palace, I felt so alone and unhappy. It
didn't matter what new party I went to or what new clothes
and jewels I received. The emptiness inside of me didn't
change.

Then one day I heard some of the servants talking about
Yahweh, the true God of our nation. How I loved to hear
their stories. I asked them how I could learn more. I was told

I must speak to the priests of Levite. Here I learned about a God who cared for His people. Why could my family not see how their lives were filled with hatred and lusting after their own desires? They had no true joy in their lives.

I began to meet with a priest named Jehoiada. I began to love God and also to love the man who taught me about Him. I went to my brother, Ahaziah, and asked to be given to Jehoiada as a wife. My father had died, and my brother was king. My stepmother was very angry and said, "Whoever heard of a princess marrying a priest?!" But my brother said he didn't care as long as I didn't expect a large dowry. I didn't want any of those riches. I just wanted to love and serve Jehoiada. Athaliah, my stepmother, said she didn't want to have anything to do with anyone who didn't serve Baal and that I shouldn't expect anything from her. Oh, how sad! Yet I felt such joy and anticipation in my new life.

Suddenly, news came to me of my brother's death. Some of my old servants came to the temple to tell me and to also say that Athaliah was angry and vowing to become queen of Judah and be in power. I could not see how this could happen because there were many grandsons of my brother to take over the reign of Judah.

That night, two of my servants ran screaming to me. "She's killing them, she is killing them all!" Surely this was not possible. Jehoiada and I ran to the palace. It was total chaos. It was true; Athaliah was having all of the grandsons put to death. There would be no one left in the royal line except her. How could I stop this? Then I remembered little Joash, who had just been born. Maybe she wouldn't remember him. I had my servants sneak me into the palace and I took baby Joash and his wet nurse with me to the temple. She would never go there. She hated God and only worshipped Baal. Jehoiada and I hid Joash with us in the temple. Athaliah made herself queen. She was power hungry, greedy, and heartless. When Joash turned seven, Jehoiada brought some leaders into the temple and introduced them to Joash, whose mother was Zibiah. Joash means "given by the Lord." Athaliah was overthrown and put to death. Joash, my nephew, became king, thus saving the lineage of David.

Remember, my name is Jehosheba. My name means "she who worships or swears by Jehovah." Isn't it amazing I was named this considering I came from a family of Baal worshippers? It demonstrates the sovereignty of God. Also, my life proves we must all make our own decisions about who we will serve. I choose to worship the true God. Have you made this choice? If you have, what mission does God want you to do to show others who you serve?

When Athaliah the mother of Ahaziah saw that her son was dead, she rose and destroyed all the royal offspring. But Jehosheba, the daughter of King Joram, sister of Ahaziah, took Joash, the son of Ahaziah, and stole him from among the king's sons who were being put to death, and placed him and his nurse in the bedroom. So they hid him from Athaliah, and he was not put to death. So he was hidden with her in the house of the Lord six years, while Athaliah was reigning over the land. Now in the seventh year Jehoiada sent and brought the captains of hundreds of the Carites and of the guard and brought them to him in the house of the Lord. Then he made a covenant with them and put them under oath in the house of the Lord, and showed them the king's son.

2 Kings 11:1-4

Verses of the Day: Psalm 46:1 and 2

God is our refuge and strength,
A very present help in trouble.

Therefore we will not fear, though the earth should
    change,
And though the mountains slip into the heart of the
    sea...

"A Trusting Woman"

Our lives sometimes come to the point where we just don't see how we are going to make it. We feel defeated. Just wait; God has the answer. Watch as God shows us how He met a desperate woman's need not just once, but twice.

I was searching outdoors for sticks. I just needed a few to make a fire so I could bake some little cakes. It had not rained for months, and the land was in a famine. I had a son, but my husband was dead. What was I to do? There was only a smidgen of flour left. Oh, where was it?

Have you ever been in a time of desperation? I lived in an area called Zarephath. *Zarephath* means "to refine" or "to test." The name sure fit my life. Just keep listening to my story and you'll understand. Zarephath was a city where most of the people worshipped Baal, but I didn't see that Baal was helping at all. I had heard much about the prophets of the Jews. They seemed to have much power, but I didn't see help coming from anywhere.

Anyway, to get back to my story. There I was searching for sticks when a man came to me. I recognized him as a prophet from the Israel nation. He wanted some water, so

I started to get it when he called out and said he wanted a piece of bread.

Now I told him, "As the Lord your God lives, I have no bread, only a handful of flour in the bowl and a little oil in the jar. I am gathering sticks, and then I am going in to prepare a cake for me and my son that we may eat it and die."

Then he said to me. "Do not fear; go, do as you have said, but make me a little bread cake from it first and bring it out to me, and afterward you may make some for yourself and for your son. For Thus says the Lord God of Israel, 'the bowl of flour shall not be exhausted, nor shall the jar of oil be empty, until the day that the Lord sends rain on the face of the earth.'"

"He must be the prophet Elijah," I thought. I had heard his God was great. But where would he get more flour and oil? With the famine, flour and oil were scarce, and if you could find them, they were very costly. Prophets weren't rich. I knew that. What was I to do? This flour and oil was all I had. Should I trust Elijah and his God? I decided it wouldn't hurt to try him and see if what he said was true. My son and I were going to die anyway. So I did as he requested and baked him a cake and took it to him first. I didn't think there would be much left for me and my son. You can imagine my amazement when I went back to the bowl of flour and flask of oil only to find them full again. I looked up. I looked under the table and everywhere. Where did it come from? I looked at Elijah and he looked up from eating his cake and smiled. His God was great and kept His promise to provide. And He continued to provide. Just what we needed for each day was in the flour bowl and oil flask. God supplied our needs. I thought I was pretty safe now. I had a prophet staying with me and I had food every day.

You'll never believe what happened next. My son became ill and then died. How could this happen? I did everything Elijah asked. Why was I being punished? Why had Elijah come to my home? I ran to him and asked him why he had come to my place and drawn God's attention to me and my sins. Why had he saved my son from starvation just to take him by an illness? Elijah came and took my son and went to an upper room in the house and laid him on his own bed. I was so devastated. I heard Elijah cry out to his God. Then I saw Elijah come down from his upper room. He was carrying my son. But my son who was dead was moving! He was alive! Elijah handed my son to me and said, "See, your son is alive!" I stood there holding my son and crying. This time I was crying for joy. This was the second time in my life I was in total desperation and the Lord saw my need and answered it with amazing results. I told Elijah I knew he was a man from God and that what he spoke was the truth. I wasn't an Israelite, yet their God was my God, too. He loved me in spite of my sin and met my needs. Please learn that from my life. God loves you and will take care of your needs even when they seem impossible. He knows. He cares. He will answer.

> But I say to you in truth, there were many widows in Israel in the days of Elijah, when the sky was shut up for three years and six months, when a great famine came over all the land; and yet Elijah was sent to none of them, but only to Zarephath, in the land of Sidon, to a woman who was a widow.
>
> Luke 4:25 and 26

Verses of the Day: Psalm 17:5 and 6

My steps have held fast to Thy paths.
My feet have not slipped.
I have called upon Thee, for Thou wilt answer me,
O God. Incline Thine ear to me, hear my speech.

"A Listening Woman"

Finding the reason why we are here on earth is so important. Sometimes we struggle to really grasp onto this reason. Listen as Huldah tells her story of how she finally got her answer.

Are you having a busy day? That's the way I felt. It just seemed like my days were going by so fast, and I didn't seem to be getting what I wanted done. I thought there just had to be more to life than this. Oh, my name is Huldah. It means "weasel." maybe because I tried to "weasel" out of doing things. I wasn't trying to get out of doing things; I just wanted to find a meaning for what I did. I needed to find some reason for living. Have you ever found yourself in this situation? I was just tired of life and doing seemingly meaningless things and going through the routine. I got married to Shallum, and I thought this would solve my problem. At first it was great, but I soon found myself in routines again. They were just a different kind. Where was I to find a reason for living? It wasn't in myself, my husband, or my family. I was looking for satisfaction in all the wrong places. Then I found some scrolls. And I started reading. They spoke of God and the wonders He had performed for my people. How had we gotten so far away from Him?! As I read, I found the answer to the meaning of my life. I realized all what my God had done for me. He took me out of slavery and bondage. Why had I forgotten His Word and done sinful things? I started reading and being alone with God each day.

One day as I was reading, God spoke to me. You can imagine my amazement! How marvelous to be able to hear from God. I told everyone what God had said. He brought me close to Him. My husband, Shallum, encouraged me to spend time with God. This was the meaning to life. I had a relationship with the One who made life. This relationship was the most important thing in my life. Let me ask you this: what is the most important relationship in your life? Everything fell into place. I was busier than I had ever been, but now I had my reason. It was all about Him. I saw life in a whole new way, and I had so much joy. People would come to me for advice. I didn't have the answers, but I knew who did. I would spend time with God, and He spoke to me. I became a prophetess. I was a speaker, a messenger for God. But it only worked if I took time and was alone with God and listened to Him. Let me ask you another question. When was the last time you were alone with God and listened to Him? This life of mine became full and busy but certainly not routine.

One day I saw several priests and scribes come to my home. What could they want? I thought I was in trouble with the king. Josiah was the king. The priest and scribes had come to me to hear what God had to say about the nation of Israel and what was to happen to them. You see, Josiah had read the Book of the Law and realized how badly the nation of Israel had disobeyed God. He knew there would be a consequence for this disobedience. God told me to tell them that because they had forsaken God and worshipped other gods, they would bring much calamity and destruction upon themselves.

Remember, my husband was Shallum. His name meant "retribution." This meant a "justly deserved penalty." And this was exactly what would happen to the nation of Israel. But because Josiah genuinely repented and humbled himself before God, God said this would not happen until after Josiah died. This was so Josiah would not have to witness the destruction of his people. You see, Josiah read the law and realized the people had sinned against God, and he prayed to God for mercy. This gave Josiah some hope. And guess what? If you read my story in the Holy Book, you'll have seen the name Tikvah. He was my husband's father. His name meant "hope."

It is marvelous how God gives meaning to our lives. I started out just frustrated and not knowing what to do. I wasn't enjoying life or looking with anticipation for each new day. Then I stopped and read His Law and listened to Him. Suddenly, my life was so full I was shouting for joy. It was only after I listened to God that He was able to use me. I was a prophetess; just ordinary me. Can you imagine what He can do for you if you'll just read His Word and listen? My desire is that you learn from my life and not be discouraged but enlightened with what God can do for you.

"Go, inquire of the Lord for me and the people and all Judah concerning the words of this book that has been found, for great is the wrath of the Lord that burns against us, because our fathers have not listened to the words of this book, to do according to all that is written concerning us." So Hilkiah the priest, Ahikam, Achbor, Shaphan, and Asaiah went to Huldah the prophetess, the wife of Shallum the son of Tikvah, the son of Harhas, keeper of the wardrobe (now she lives in Jerusalem in the Second Quarter); and they spoke to her.

2 Kings 22:13 and 14

29

Verses of the Day: Psalm 13:5 and 6

But I have trusted in your loving-kindness.
My heart shall rejoice in Your salvation.
I will sing to the Lord because He has dealt bountifully
with me.

"A Grieving Woman"

~~~

Have you ever wondered if God really knows or cares about what is going on in your life? Here is proof that Jesus cares, and not only that, but He also has the answer to whatever circumstance comes our way. Listen as this lady of Nain tells her story.

It started as a dark day for me. It seemed like one tragedy after another was happening to me. I didn't see how I was going to continue on with my life. My husband had died and now only my son and I were left. My son was such a help to me and was my hope for the future. Suddenly, my son became ill and died. And here you find me walking behind my son's coffin. There were other mourners with me as well as the men who carried the coffin. I was weeping. It seemed like I had cried so much that there couldn't be any tears left. Have you ever come to such a time in your life where you feel there is no hope?

There I was, getting ready to bury my son. We were walking slowly out of the town of Nain. I saw another group come toward us and I thought they were going to pass. But they stopped and one of the men came toward me. I looked up at Him, and He came and said to me, "Do not weep." He had such kind eyes, and I could see He was trying to console me. "How nice of Him," I thought. I did not know this man, and I had not said anything to Him. Yet here He was. He wanted to share my sorrow. Yet all of a sudden He touched the coffin. Everyone stopped and gasped. We all knew it was against our custom to touch the coffin. You would be considered "unclean." Why was He touching the coffin? I knew He was trying to help, but I wished He would just leave me alone with my suffering. I just wanted to get finished with the task at hand. Then He spoke again. It was astonishing what He said. He spoke to my son in the coffin. He said, "Young man, I say to you arise!" Can you imagine our amazement when my son rose up and spoke?! My son who was dead was now alive! The men carrying the coffin were so amazed they dropped the coffin! We laughed and cried and jumped for joy. Who was this man that He could raise the dead? He was from Galilee and His name was Jesus. His disciples were with Him, and they, too, marveled at what Jesus had done. I thought, "He must be a great prophet, but no, He must be the promised Messiah. I am just known as the widow of Nain." I wasn't anyone special, yet Jesus saw my need even without me saying a word. He saw my tears and met my need. I no longer had tears of sorrow but rather tears of joy. My son and I hugged and I kissed Him. We wanted to learn more about Jesus and His teachings. The people who were with us were glorifying God. Everyone was running and telling what Jesus had done. A day starting in darkness ended in joyous light.

You'll remember I am from the city of Nain. *Nain* means "beauty." I couldn't see any beauty until I met Jesus. He put hope and beauty back into my life. He wants to do the same for you. Jesus sees your despair and wants to give you peace. It may not be death. It could be any situation in your life that is hurting you. Jesus says, "Don't weep." He has the answer that will bring joy back into your life.

Soon afterwards he went to a city called Nain; and His disciples were going along with Him, accompanied by a large crowd. Now as he approached the gate of the city, a dead man was being carried out, the only son of his mother, and she was a widow; and a sizeable crowd from the city was with her. When the Lord saw her, He felt compassion for her, and said to her, "Do not weep." And He came up and touched the coffin; and the bearers came to a halt. And He said, "Young man, I say to you, arise!" The dead man sat up and began to speak. And Jesus gave him back to his mother.

Luke 7: 11-15

Verses of the Day: Psalm 9:1 and 2

I will give thanks to the Lord with all my heart;
I will tell all Thy wonders.
I will be glad and exalt in Thee;
I will sing praise to Thy name, O Most High.

"A Certain Woman"

—⌒⌒—

Feel the breeze and smell the salt in the air. Yes, we are on the seacoast. We are in the City of Capernaum. A lady here has an exciting story to tell.

Hello, I am delighted to be telling you my story. Actually, my story has been told three times. Matthew, Mark, and Luke wrote about me in their books in the Bible. They never gave my name. I was just "a certain woman." I could have been called Mara. That means "sad." Let me explain. I am going to take you back to 28 A.D., to the city of Capernaum. This is where I was living when my life changed. The city's name means "city of Nahum," and *Nahum* means "compassion." Capernaum is in the Galilee area and is on the seacoast. It is where Jesus did most of His miracles. He showed His compassion in the city of compassion. Isn't it marvelous how the Master has everything planned?! But I digress. Let me get back to my story.

My life was going along fine until I suddenly started hemorrhaging. I just thought it was my normal time, but it wouldn't stop. Now during our time and according to our Levitical law (Lev.15:25-33), a woman was considered unclean during this time. We were not to touch or be touched by anyone. Anyone who touched us was considered unclean. I went to many physicians and tried all their remedies. All they did was take my money. I tried everything! Still, I would not stop hemorrhaging. No one would touch me. No one wanted anything to do with me. I was so depressed! This went on for twelve years. Can you imagine how I felt? I was very lonely, and I didn't think anyone understood what I was going through. I just wanted to die and end all the pain.

Then I heard about a man named Jesus. He was performing miracles and healing people. The more I heard, the more I knew that if I could just touch the fringe of His cloak, I would be healed. After hearing He was returning to Capernaum, I ran to the seashore to wait for Him. It was very crowded. Everyone was pushing and shoving. I was frightened I would not be able to reach Him. I saw a leader from the synagogue approach Jesus. He was asking for Jesus to help his daughter. I thought, "Who am I that Jesus would speak to me? I am not anyone important." Oh, but I knew I had to get to Him and touch Him. That shouldn't bother Him. I would come up behind Jesus. No one would notice me. So I pushed, shoved, and crawled. Finally, I saw the fringe of His cloak.

Let me pause and explain to you about the fringe on His cloak. It was the law given by Moses (Numbers 15:37-41) that our cloaks would be made with tassels or fringe on the corners of the cloak. On each of the tassels would be a cord of blue. The tassels would help us remember all the commandments of the Lord so as to do them and not follow after our own hearts and our own eyes. We were to remember to do all God's commandments and be holy to God. To touch the fringe was to touch everything about God.

Now, to get back to my story. I leaned forward and touched the fringe of His cloak. Actually, the word is *haptomai*, which means "to fasten onto" or "to grasp." I was in despair. This was the only hope I had for release from my hemorrhaging, which would give me the chance to keep living. It is hard to describe what happened next. I felt a surge of power (*dunamis*) go throughout my body. I believe you get your word *dynamite* from this word. Instantly, the hemorrhaging stopped. Jesus cleansed me of the flow of blood. Leviticus 12:7 talks about the priest making a sacrifice for the woman at this time for atonement and cleansing. Jesus was my atonement and cleansing. But wait! Oh, my! Jesus stopped walking and turned around. He asked, "Who touched me?" I heard Peter and the followers say they hadn't touched Him, but that there were people all around. Surely, many were touching Him. I was so frightened! I tried to crouch down so no one would notice me. I heard Jesus say someone had purposely touched Him because He had felt His power go from Him. I knew I had to tell Him I had touched Him. I came close and fell down at His feet. As I looked into His eyes, I could see His love and compassion. I didn't have to tell Him who I was. He knew. I explained to all the people around me the reason why I had sought out Jesus and touched Him. I shouted out that I was healed! I will never forget the words Jesus said to me: "Daughter, your faith has made you (whole) well; go in peace." The Master called me "daughter"! I had had no one who wanted to claim me for twelve years, and here He was calling me His daughter. I didn't know it then, but I now know I was the only individual Jesus called by this endearment. He knew how much I needed that reassurance of love and acceptance. When He said, "Hath made you whole or well," He used the word *sozo*, which means "to save" or "deliverance." He didn't just deliver me from my physical infirmity; He delivered me from my spiritual iniquity. He told me to "go in peace." My life had been one big turmoil; now, He gave me peace. This was a continuous peace, not just for that moment but forever!

When I look back at my experience, I am amazed. I reached out and touched Jesus. I stopped bleeding immediately. Think about all the blood that was shed for atonement before Jesus. After Jesus and His blood on the cross, the shedding of blood was instantly stopped. He was the answer for our atonement. He is my Messiah, my God. He took my life and made it worth living. I was brought from a life of pain, sorrow, and emptiness to a life filled with peace, joy, and service to Him. My eyes were brought off my circumstances and were placed or fixed upon Him. Was my life perfect and without problems? No, but I always had His peace in my heart to help me through. And now I spend eternity with Him. At the beginning of my story, I could have been called "Mara," but now I can be called Mehetable, which means "God makes happy." Does your life seem in despair, empty, or lonely? Touch the fringe of His garment. Go to Jesus. He can change your life!

> And a woman who had a hemorrhage for twelve years, and could not be healed by anyone, came up behind Him and touched the fringe of His cloak; and immediately her hemorrhage stopped. And Jesus said, "Who is the one who touched Me?" And while they were all denying it, Peter said, "Master, the multitudes are crowding and pressing upon You." But Jesus said, "Someone did touch Me, for I was aware that power had gone out of Me." And when the woman saw that she had not escaped notice, she came trembling and fell down before Him, and declared in the presence of all the people the reason why she had touched Him, and how she had been immediately healed. And He said to her, "Daughter, your faith has made you well; go in peace."
>
> Luke 8:43-48

Verses of the Day: Psalm 18:1 and 2

"I love Thee, O Lord, my strength."
The Lord is my rock and my fortress and my deliverer,
My God, my rock, in whom I take refuge;
My shield and the horn of my salvation, my stronghold.

"A Risen Woman"

W e are traveling today to a city called Jaffa. It is a seaport city on the Mediterranean Sea. In biblical times, the city was called Joppa, meaning "beautiful." As it was only thirty-eight miles from Jerusalem, many of the disciples would go around this area to teach about Jesus. Peter was in a city called Lydda, which was only about twelve miles from Joppa. Let me have our next lady tell her story.

Joppa was an interesting city in which to live. I was blessed with a Jewish mother and a Greek father. Therefore, I had two names: Dorcas, Greek for "gazelle," and Tabitha, Hebrew for "gazelle." In my time, a gazelle was a symbol of elegant grace and beauty. Now, I wasn't beautiful, but they wanted me to learn that true beauty came from a person's actions and words, not necessarily from their outward appearance. My father arranged a very wonderful marriage for me. He was a tailor and had a very profitable business in Joppa. Oh, but better yet, he was a follower of Jesus' teachings, and soon I became a disciple, too. I thought my life was set. I sewed with my husband and shared in his work, and we worshipped Jesus together. But then my husband became ill and died. My parents were dead, my husband was dead, and I had no children so I was all alone. I sold my husband's business, which made me financially secure. I kept on going to the worship services and learning more about Jesus. While there, I would see many widows and hear about their struggles. My heart went out to them, but how could I help? I prayed for the Lord to show me how to help these women and to share with them about Jesus. I knew I could live on a little less and give more in the offering. It wasn't much, but it would help. What else could I do? All I knew how to do was sew.

Then one day as I was worshipping, I looked at some of these widows and saw the ragged clothes they were wearing. It suddenly occurred to me I could sew them some clothes. I knew where I could get the supplies at a really reasonable price. It was wonderful to see their faces when I gave them a tunic or a coat. I would tell them about how Jesus loved them. I made the clothes and gave them to anyone in need, even to those who had never attended a worship service to hear about Jesus. Oh, how wonderful it was to see their faces now full of hope!

One day I fell ill. I just couldn't get out of bed. I thought, "I'll be better tomorrow," but I kept feeling ill. Then I just closed my eyes. Now what I tell you next was told to me because I was dead and I felt a wonderful peace. But some of my widow friends told me about the next happenings. Some of the widows had washed my body and dressed it and placed it in the upper room. Some of the worshippers knew Peter was in the next city, and they ran to tell him I was dead. They were upset at my death. This makes me feel very honored. You must think about this. How would people feel about your death?

Peter hurried to the house and saw the many widows. They were crying and showing Peter all of the clothes I had made for them. Peter was moved by their words and told them to leave the room. Peter knelt and prayed. I heard my name, "Tabitha." It was my Hebrew name. My mother had always called me Tabitha. But there I heard my name and a command I knew I must obey. I heard, "Tabitha, arise." I opened my eyes, and there was Peter kneeling beside me. He smiled and I smiled back. He took my hand, and I sat up. I was alive again! Although I was happy where I was, God had other plans for me. I rejoiced with the widows as I walked down to the other room. They couldn't believe I was alive again. I explained that we had an all-powerful God. Peter stayed in town a few days just to help minister to these young believers. I didn't want to go through the dying process again, but I knew my Lord wanted me to keep serving Him as well as being a testimony a little while longer. So I kept sewing and telling everyone I saw about my miracle. Many believed in the Lord. I was given a chance to live anew for the Lord. My, what a miracle! What a mighty God we serve! Our Lord knows our hearts and our needs. We must listen and obey Him.

Now in Joppa there was a certain disciple named Tabitha (which translated in Greek is called Dorcas); this woman was abounding with deeds of kindness and charity, which she continually did. And it came about at that time that she fell sick and died; and when they had washed her body, they had laid it in an upper room. And since Lydda was near Joppa, the disciples, having heard that Peter was there, sent two men to him, entreating him. "Do not delay to come to us." And Peter arose and went with them. And when he had come, they brought him into the upper room; and all the widows stood beside him weeping, and showing all the tunics and garments that Dorcas used to make while she was with them. But Peter sent them all out and knelt down and prayed, and turning to the body, he said, "Tabitha, arise." And she opened her eyes, and when she saw Peter, she sat up. And he gave her his hand and raised her up; and calling the saints and widows, he presented her alive. And it became known all over Joppa, and many believed in the Lord. And it came about that he stayed many days in Joppa with a certain tanner, Simon.

Acts 9: 36-43

Verse of the Day: Psalm 143:8

"Let me to hear Thy loving- kindness in the morning;
For I trust in Thee;
Teach me the way in which I should walk;
For to Thee I lift up my soul.

"A Determined Woman"

C an someone who has sinned still be useful to God? Many think that because of their past sins, they can't do anything for the Lord. Read and see how God proves them wrong.

Here I was walking around with a piece of a red cord in my hand. I did this as a reminder of what God did for me. Yes, you know who I am. I am Rahab. Now, don't say it! I heard you! All right, I am known as Rahab the harlot. I would prefer for you to think of me as just "Rahab." How would you like to be called Linda the liar or Gloria the gossiper?! It is not pleasant to always be called by your past sins, yet it serves as another reminder of where I was and what God did for me.

Let me explain. There I was in Jericho being an innkeeper. One side of my inn was actually part of the wall of Jericho. I was a prostitute. That's how I earned my living in order to support my family.

One day two men came to my establishment. I knew they were foreigners. I had heard about the Israelites and how their God was helping them to destroy their enemies. I knew these two men were being sought by the king. I had to make a choice. Did I give them to the king or help them? I believed their God was mightier than my king. So I quickly hid them. I knew the Israelites would be coming soon to kill us and destroy Jericho, so after the king's men left, I went up to my roof, which was where I hid them, and began to bargain with them. I told them I would show them how to safely get out of Jericho if they could promise to save me and my family. They agreed and told me to hang a red cord outside my window on the wall. When the Israelites saw the red cord, they would not harm us. I was so excited. We were going to be saved. I explained to my family that they were to get their things ready and come to my inn when I gave them the word. Then I waited…and waited…and waited. Have you ever waited on God? You know He is going to save you from a situation, but you have to wait for God's timing.

Then the word came. The Israelites were camped outside the wall of Jericho. I quickly sent word to my family. I checked to make sure the red cord was outside my window. The Israelites walked around the city. I thought, "This is good. Joshua and his men are trying to find the best way into the city." The next day they did it again. They walked around the city. Then the next day they did it again! What was Joshua doing? I could hear the people of Jericho getting more and more nervous and upset. But I kept my door closed and my family inside my inn. Again I went to check the red cord in my window just to make sure it was still there. The next day the Israelites walked around the city. Maybe this was a new exercise program to get in shape for battle? They walked around the city for six days in a row. I was so confused. I knew I had to trust and wait.

On the seventh day, the Israelites started walking…and they walked…and they walked. I thought, "These poor people are going to be so exhausted, they won't be able to hold a sword." After they had walked around seven times, I heard a loud noise! Then there was screaming and the ground was trembling. We could hear the walls of Jericho falling. Then there was silence. A knock came on the door. I opened the door and there was Joshua and the two spies I had hidden. I and my family were safe. They had kept their promise as God always keeps His promises.

Now that was great, but it gets better. The Israelites allowed us to go with them outside their camp, of course. But one of the spies, Salmon, came to visit me often. He was so kind and nice. He took me as his wife. Can you believe that?! Here I was, a harlot. Someone who should have been stoned. Yet here was a man who loved me and knew I had given up my past and wanted to worship the God of Israel. When God does something, He does it in a big way! We had a son and named him Boaz. You may remember he was the one who loved and married Ruth. He had learned from his father to look at the heart and not at the outside circumstances of a woman.

Many times later in the Holy Bible, my story is mentioned. Yet every time I am called Rahab the harlot. They couldn't forget my past. Oh, but there is one place where I am just Rahab (Matthew 1:5). It is in the lineage of Jesus Christ. You see, God had forgiven me and saw my sin no more. Even today, God can do the same for you!

> By faith Rahab the harlot did not perish along with those who were disobedient, after she had welcomed the spies in peace.
>
> Hebrews 11:31

Verse of the Day: Psalm 19:14

> Let the words of my mouth and the meditation of my heart
> Be acceptable in Thy sight,
> O Lord, my rock and my Redeemer.

"A Broken, Contrite Woman"

Praise and worship the King! Why are we ashamed to say "hallelujah" or "praise the Lord" in public? Our Lord, who has done so much for us, is worthy of our outward praise. Read and see how a woman unashamedly shows her gratefulness to our Lord.

Shalom. I am delighted to tell you my story. You will find it in the Gospels. They never gave my name. I am just unknown. Let me start at the beginning. There was a very unique gathering happening at Simon the Pharisee's house, and I wanted to go. I dressed up and took my most valued possession, an alabaster box filled with costly perfume. You see, a very special person was going to attend whom I wanted to meet. His name was Jesus. I had heard Him teach and say, "Come unto me all ye who are heavy laden and I will give you rest." Rest! I had so much failure and unrest in my life! But here was someone who said He could give me a new life. I was a prostitute, but a very high-class one. I was considered very successful in my profession. I was seeking love, acceptance, and importance in all the wrong ways. My heart was in turmoil and I had no peace or real happiness. As I heard Jesus, I repented and determined to lead a new life.

It was difficult to find another way of making a living, but I was seeking happiness in the right way.

I knew Simon wouldn't invite me. He was a very prestigious Pharisee, and I was considered a very sinful woman. It was our custom that even if you weren't invited to the house, you could come and stand around the walls of the house and watch as they dined. So there I was at a home where I wasn't invited or wanted. Simon frowned at me, for he knew of my past. There He was! Jesus! He reclined at the table with His feet extended away from the table, as was our way of dining. As I saw and listened to Him, I started to think back to how my life used to be. Here was the One who gave me hope and release from the bondage I was in. Oh, how much I loved Him! How grateful I was, and with a broken heart I started to weep. I was so embarrassed as I saw my tears fall on His feet. I opened my alabaster box and knelt down at His feet and poured out the perfume on them. I didn't have anything to wipe His feet with, so I unloosened my hair and wiped them with my hair. Can you imagine?! I held the Master's feet. With a contrite heart, I wanted to show Jesus how I adored Him. I didn't know it, but Simon was watching me with disgust. He was thinking that if Jesus knew what kind of woman I was, Jesus wouldn't let me touch Him. Jesus knew what He was thinking. He began to tell Simon a story.

He said, "Simon, there was a moneylender who was owed by two debtors. One owed him five hundred denarii and the other fifty denarii. They couldn't pay, so the moneylender graciously forgave them both. So which of them will love him more?"

Simon replied, "I suppose the one who He forgave more."

I heard Jesus say, "You have judged correctly." But then He turned toward me! I was so embarrassed! I just wanted to sink! Everyone was looking at me! Jesus said, "Simon, do you see this woman? I entered your house and you gave

Me no water for My feet, but she has wet My feet with her tears and wiped them with her hair. You gave Me no kiss of greeting, but she has kissed My feet. You did not anoint My head with oil, but she has anointed My feet with perfume. For this reason I say to you her sins, which are many, have been forgiven for she loved much." Then He spoke to me! He said my sins were forgiven. "Your faith has saved you; go in peace." I looked up into His eyes. There was so much love and compassion there. He was my Lord, my Messiah, and He cared about me, someone who was so unworthy. He restored me to the grace and beauty He had intended for me. Do you know He cares that much for you, too? Come to Him with a broken heart and He will forgive you and give you a new life. Where you have no peace, He will give you rest and joy.

> Now one of the Pharisees was requesting Him to dine with him. And He entered the Pharisee's house, and reclined at the table. And behold, there was a woman in the city who was a sinner; and when she learned that He was reclining at the table in the Pharisee's house, she brought an alabaster vial of perfume, and standing behind Him at His feet, weeping, she began to wet His feet with her tears, and kept wiping them with the hair of her head, and kissing His feet, and anointing them with the perfume. Now when the Pharisee who had invited Him saw this, he said to himself, "If this man were a prophet He would know who and what sort of a person this woman is who is touching Him, that she is a sinner." And Jesus answered and said to him, "Simon, I have something to say to you." And he replied, "Say it Teacher." "A certain moneylender had two debtors: one owed five hundred denarii, and the other fifty. "When they were unable to repay, he graciously forgave them

both. Which of them therefore will love him more?" Simon answered and said, "I suppose the one whom he forgave more." And He said to him, "You have judged correctly." And turning toward the woman, He said to Simon, "Do you see this woman? I entered your house; you gave Me no water for My feet, but she has wet My feet with her tears, and wiped them with her hair. "You gave Me no kiss; but she, since the time I came in, has not ceased to kiss My feet. "You did not anoint My head with oil, but she anointed My feet with perfume. "For this reason I say to you, her sins, which are many, have been forgiven, for she loved much; but he who is forgiven little, loves little." And He said to her, "Your sins have been forgiven."

Luke 7:36-48

Verses of the Day: Psalm 25:4 and 5

Make me know Thy ways, O Lord;
Teach me Thy paths.
Lead me in Thy truth and teach me,
For Thou art the God of my salvation;
For Thee I wait all the day.

"A Hidden Woman"

Have you ever wondered what is or will be required of us to serve the Lord? We waste so much of our day serving our own wants and desires, yet we don't often think about serving Christ and just what this will cost us. Listen as a lady tells a story about her husband and herself and just what it cost them to serve Jesus Christ.

There he went again, "Jesus this and Jesus that." That was all my husband could talk about. He came home from work one day and all he could talk about was a man he met who was called Jesus. What I wanted to know was where were the fish he was supposed to bring home for supper! I couldn't imagine anyone could be of so much importance that Peter would forget the fish. But as I began listening to Peter and saw his enthusiasm, I began to want to see this man myself. Peter told me this man "Jesus" was the answer to our nation's oppression. And, sure enough, the moment I met Jesus and looked into His eyes, I knew He was the answer to everything! Peter wanted to follow Jesus and learn from Him. It meant I must look after our home and business, but I was willing. I was willing because I knew this was what my husband must do. Sometimes God asks us to do hard tasks in order for His work to be done. We must be willing to answer this kind of calling. I learned to develop a serving heart. Before Jesus came into my life, I wanted Peter to bring in the finances and serve me. I soon learned I must have a servant's heart and see to the needs of those around me.

Then one day my mother who lived with us became ill with a very high fever. I sent word to Peter, who was with Jesus and some of the disciples. As soon as Jesus heard, He came to our home. He went into the room where my mother lay and took her by the hand and healed her. It was so amazing! Here she was, close to death, and the next minute she was in the kitchen yelling at me to help her cook a meal for Jesus and the others with Him. During the next few days, I watched Him heal many and cast out demons in others. I thought life couldn't get any better.

Oh, how wrong I was! Things got extremely bad before they became better. For three and a half years, my husband followed the Lord. Sometimes the other women and I traveled with Peter and the other apostles, caring for their needs as they served the Master. Then one night word came that Jesus had been arrested by the Romans and crucified. Peter was devastated and kept repeating, "I denied Him, I denied Him; when He needed me most, I denied Him."

John came to our home. It was the third day since Jesus had been crucified, and Peter went with John to the tomb where Jesus had been buried. I don't remember a time when I was so upset. I couldn't even think about what the future was going to be. I just sat and cried. Then Peter came and said Jesus' body was gone! What were we to do! Peter said he was going back to fishing and that we would wait to see what would happen next. Well, we didn't wait long.

Several days later, Peter came in and said, "Guess who fed me breakfast this morning?!" He didn't even give me a chance to guess before he shouted, "Jesus! He is risen from the dead! He's alive, and He ate with us!" I couldn't believe it. Then I remembered Jesus had said He was going to do this, but I didn't understand what He was saying at the time.

Just think about all the promises Jesus has made to us. Why are we so shocked when He fulfills these promises? I had been so upset only to find out Jesus had everything under control all the time. I certainly learned a lesson here. I now know that no matter the situation, Jesus has His own way of handling it. I simply needed to trust Him.

Peter said we needed to go to an upper room and wait. I wasn't sure what we were to wait for because Jesus had ascended to heaven. I simply obeyed, and there we were, one hundred and twenty of us, waiting. Suddenly, I heard and felt a rushing wind and saw clouds of fire. It was so astonishing and hard to explain. I heard everyone speaking and everyone understanding what was being said in their own language. People were saying we had too much wine. Then I heard my husband speak. I had never heard him speak with so much confidence before. I was afraid and yet so proud. My husband was a different man and I was changed, too. His life was now dedicated to preaching and teaching about Jesus wherever he could. My life was to be spent helping my husband. Sometimes I traveled with him, and at other times I managed the affairs at home.

Then came the time when we were arrested and put in a Roman jail. I was afraid and cold and tired. I wondered, "Where are You, Jesus?" Then I felt His presence and I could hear Him in my heart saying, "I'm right here with you; I have never left you." I felt such peace. Even though my circumstances were unchanged, I felt so different. As they came to get me, I knew I was going to die. Peter tried to comfort me and said, "Remember the Lord." I gave him a shaky smile and nodded. I was killed because I believed in Jesus. The moment I closed my eyes to this world was the moment I was reunited with my Savior, my Master!

In your walk with the Lord, you will never know what will be required of you. Are you prepared? I was honored to be chosen as one who would die for Him as a testimony for others. Think about what Jesus has chosen you to do in order to be a testimony for Him.

> And when Jesus had come to Peter's home, He saw his mother-in-law lying sick in bed with fever. And He touched her hand, and the fever left; and she arose, and waited on Him. And when evening had come, they brought to Him many who were demon-possessed; and He cast out the spirits with a word, and healed all who were ill in order that what was spoken through Isaiah the prophet might be fulfilled, saying "He Himself took our infirmities and carried away our diseases."
>
> Matthew 8:14-18

Verse of the Day: Psalm 27:1

The Lord is my light and my salvation;
Whom shall I fear?
The Lord is the defense of my life;
Whom shall I dread?

"A Humble Woman"

So much of this world is dangerous to our children. We must be watchful and keep our children safe from the evil influences around them. But what happens when one of them gets caught up in this world and is in trouble? Do we give up in despair? See one woman's answer to this question.

My situation can't get any worse. Here I am living in a Syro-Phoenician city that is full of sin. It seems like everyone is into demonism and witchcraft. One of my daughter's friends convinced her to become involved in some witchcraft games, and now my daughter is demon-possessed. What am I to do? The many so-called gods we worship do absolutely nothing. How can I help my daughter? I have even thought about killing my daughter and myself, thus releasing her from the demon. I am so scared.

Then I hear about a man named Jesus. He is healing people, and demons obey Him when He tells them to come out. He surely is the only help for my daughter. I hear He is on His way to my area, which is between Tyre and Sidon. Oh, we need someone like Him to come and clean our place out. The sin is so awful and depressing. Do you know of a place like this? It just sucked my daughter up when I wasn't paying attention. Oh, how I want my sweet daughter back. I "study up" on this Jesus. He is a Jew. I am a Canaanite. Jews usually don't have anything to do with us. But I have to try.

There He is with his disciples. I cry out to Him. I cry out to His disciples. I call Him "Lord, Son of David." But He doesn't answer me. Then He makes a statement to His disciples. I hear Him say, "I was not sent except to the lost sheep of the house of Israel."

Then I come before Him and say, "Lord, help me."

He says, "It is not good to take the children's bread and throw it to the little dogs."

I know what He means. He is here to help the Israelites, not us Gentiles. But He is Lord of all, I think, so I say, "Yes, Lord, yet even the little dogs eat the crumbs that fall from their master's table." All I want is just a little from the Lord.

Then Jesus turns and looks at me. Oh, I wish you could have been there to see Him. He smiles, and his eyes are so full of love.

He says, "O, woman, great is your faith. Let it be to you as you desire."

What a great God! I turn away. I believe He has taken the demon from my daughter. I run all the way home. There she is, running to greet me with a beautiful smile on her face. She and I are hugging each other and crying. I tell her how I went to Jesus and how He made her whole again. Jesus didn't have to listen to me, and He certainly didn't have to yield to my request, yet He did.

"Oh, woman, your faith is great; be it done for you as you wish" (Matthew 15:28). How merciful and gracious is our God! Even when we are so unworthy, He still listens and answers. Do you find yourself in a situation that seems impossible? Jesus is waiting to hear from you. He will have an answer for you that will change your life.

And from there He arose and went away to the region of Tyre. And when He had entered a house, He wanted no one to know of it; yet He could not escape notice. But after hearing of Him, a woman whose little daughter had an unclean spirit, immediately came and fell at His feet. Now the woman was a Gentile, of the Syrophoenician race. And she kept asking Him to cast the demon out of her daughter. And He was saying to her, "Let the children be satisfied first, for it is not good to take the children's bread and throw it to the dogs." But she answered and said to Him, "Yes, Lord, but even the dogs under the table feed on the children's crumbs." And He said to her, "Because of this answer go your way; the demon has gone out of your daughter." And going back to her home, she found the child lying on the bed, the demon having departed.

Mark 7: 24-30

Verse of the Day: Psalm 27:14

Wait for the Lord;
Be strong, and let your heart take courage;
Yes, wait for the Lord.

"A Giving Woman"

What can we give a God who owns everything? He has been so good to us. How can we repay Him? Read and see how one woman answers this question.

"What can I give to God? It is time to go to the temple to give to the treasury. I know the Pharisees and the scribes are going to bring much to the storehouse. How can I match that kind of giving?" These are the things that kept going through my mind. I thought my life was set. I had a kind husband and several children. I was so happy. Suddenly, all of this changed when my husband died. I became a widow and my children depended on me for a living. I cleaned houses and baked bread and sold it on the street. It was hard work. Some days I was so tired I didn't see how I could make the next day. My children were growing, and it seemed they needed new shoes and clothes every day. How was I going to make it, let alone give something to the treasury?

One evening after I put the children to bed, I began to think over my life. "It has been almost five years since my husband died," I thought. "Here I am, a poor widow with children to raise. I certainly don't have any extra. But I have enough food for myself and my children. I have my health and the ability to work and earn what my family needs. I am poor, yet I am content and my children are loved and happy. I don't need the many things others have in order to be happy. It is wonderful how good God is to me." I began to think about all God had done for the Israel nation. "My, how gracious and merciful is our God! I just need to get my eyes off my circumstances and place them on God. This puts everything back into the right perspective." So that was why I was asking myself what I had to give to show God how much I loved Him. All I had was two mites left. It was all I had. I was going to use it to buy a little flour so I could bake some bread. But no, I decided I would give all I had to God. He deserves everything I have, for He has given me everything I have ever needed.

So there I was at the treasury. I thought, "Oh my, look at these people with all their fine clothes. I'll just slip in and put my two mites into the treasury and leave quickly. No one will notice me. I guess my two mites may not help much, but it's all I have. I walked up, and as I was slipping my offering in I noticed a man standing by me. I happened to look at him just as I put my mites into the box. He looked at me and smiled. I smiled back. It was such an encouragement to me. I went on to work and felt so good inside.

God was so good to me and allowed me to raise my children. I was always poor in finances but rich in the love of God. I never thought much about what I gave that day. I usually just remembered the man who had smiled. Yet I now know it was Jesus who had smiled at me. He spoke to his disciples about what I had given and He knew I had given all I had. Our God knows our circumstances. It isn't how much we give that is important. What we do with our money reveals our priorities. Our God is so good. How can we not give back to Him out of what He has provided for us? I was just a poor widow, but I hope you have learned something from my life that will encourage you the rest of your life.

And He sat down opposite the treasury, and began observing how the multitude were putting money into the treasury; and many rich people were putting in large sums. And a poor widow came and put in two small copper coins, which amount to a cent. And calling His disciples to Him, He said to them, "Truly I say to you, this poor widow put in more than all the contributors to the treasury; for they all put in out of their surplus, but she, out of her poverty, put in all she owned, all she had to live on."

Mark 12: 41-4

Verses of the Day: Psalm 16: 7, 8, and 9

I will bless the Lord who has counseled me;
Indeed, my mind instructs me in the night.
I have set the Lord continually before me;
Because He is at my right hand,
I will not be shaken.
Therefore my heart is glad, and my glory rejoices;
My flesh also will dwell securely.

"A Promised Woman"

You never know what the Lord has in store for you. God wants to do amazing things in our lives. We must learn to be obedient to His call. Sometimes we must step out on faith, not really knowing where He may lead. Listen as Sarah tells us her experience in following God's command.

There I was, having a nice breakfast, when my husband came in and joined me. He looked across the table and said, "My dear wife, you must pack, for we are going on a trip."

I said, "How nice, a little time away together."

He said, "Oh, no, we are packing up all of our possessions and moving."

"Where are we going?" I asked.

His reply was, "I don't know; God will tell us."

Now think about this. I was just calmly told we were packing up and moving and we had no idea where we were going! What would your reaction be? I think every emotion went through my mind. Yes, my name is Sarah; actually, at that time my name was Sarai, and my husband was Abram. What a morning! My whole life was being changed. Before I said something I shouldn't, I knew I had to stop and think. I knew my husband loved God and loved me; therefore, I knew I needed to just trust him. So there I was, packing up and getting ready to set off on a journey, which meant we would be living in tents. I do not like tents. They are hot and dirty.

Have you ever been in situations where you just had to trust God? Sometimes our faith needs to be tested. I didn't understand but I knew I must leave my comfort zone and go rejoicing in the Lord and trusting my husband.

Now God had told my husband he would have a son and be a father of many nations. I wanted this for my husband very much, but I hadn't been able to bear him any babies. I even laughed at the angel of the Lord when I heard him say this. I couldn't have children, I thought, so I figured I'd just help God out with His plans. Have you ever tried that? Sometimes it is hard to wait on the Lord for His timing in our lives, so we step in and try to help God out. I did. I took my handmaiden into Abram so he could have a son with her. Oh, my, was that a mistake! Unfortunately, the world is still under the consequences for my sin of unbelief. I had so much to learn about trusting and waiting on the Lord. He changed my name from Sarai to Sarah and promised to make me the mother of a nation. And, at ninety years of age, I gave birth to Isaac. His birth meant the beginning of the Jewish nation. God always fulfills His promises. Why do we have such a problem in believing Him? I lived in tents the rest of my life, following the Lord's leading of my husband. I failed many times, yet the Lord kept His promise to me. When it came my time to leave this life, my husband purchased a little piece of land for a burial plot. The Lord blessed me with 127 years on this earth, and now I have eternity with Him.

I wanted to leave this message with you that God always keeps His promises. You must trust in Him and wait for His timing. When God changed my name, I became a new person. I had a new destiny in life. When you accept the

Lord, you have a new life. Wouldn't it be nice if He changed your name, too? You have a new destiny.

> Sarah said, "God has made laughter for me; everyone who hears will laugh with me." And she said, "Who would have said to Abraham that Sarah would nurse children? Yet I have borne him a son in his old age."
>
> Genesis 21: 6 and 7

Verses of the Day: Psalm 5:2 and 3

Heed the sound of my cry for help, my King and my
    God,
For to Thee do I pray.
In the morning, O Lord Thou wilt hear my voice;
In the morning I will order my prayer to Thee and eagerly
    watch.

"A Disappointed Woman"

⁓꧁꧂⁓

To be barren (without child) after many years of marriage was an awful situation for a Jewish woman in ancient times. Here we find a woman pleading with God for a child. Let's see if this was a blessing or a curse.

There I was in prayer again, asking God to give me a child. I had been with my husband, Manoah, many years, but still I was without child. All of a sudden, an angel of the Lord appeared before me. I can tell you I was thoroughly shocked. The angel said I was to have a son. I was to dedicate him as a Nazirite to God, for he would begin to deliver Israel out of the hands of the Philistines. Talk about being surprised! I was so excited I ran and told my husband. He wanted the angel to come and tell him what to do. I prayed, and the angel came again and delivered the same message. Now, let me explain about a "Nazirite." There are three things I wasn't to do in order to show total dedication to God:

1. Don't drink wine or anything from the vine.
2. Don't be around anything dead.
3. Don't cut your hair.

Now I followed all of these rules faithfully, and I was blessed with a son. We named him Samson. I loved him so much. I wanted him to have anything he desired. I thought that was best for him. But as I look back, I see I was mistaken, for I didn't show him how to desire the things of the Lord above all things. I first recognized this when Samson came to us about taking a Philistine woman as his wife. We tried to discourage him, but he only wanted his way. So we gave in and took him to the father. You know how it is when you look back on things in life and say, "I wish I hadn't done that"? Oh, my, I wish I had done what was right instead of giving in to my son's wants. I just wanted him to have the best. But I didn't teach him to put God's will above his own. I had to watch my son make many bad choices. Oh, he was judge over Israel for twenty years just like God said he would be. But he never delivered Israel, which was God's design for him. Because of my son's disobedience, God left him in the hands of his enemies. The only thing I could do was pray that Samson would come back to the Lord. I would cry and hurt so much about the pain and sorrow my son was going through. There was nothing I could do except place him in God's hands. I knew God could bring my son back to his senses.

Have you ever been in my situation? It's where everything seems out of control. I asked for repentance and for God to rescue my son. My son was put in prison. His eyes were put out and the people mocked him. Oh, the shame of it all! Then people came running to tell me Samson had killed more than three thousand Philistines. How could this be? My other son came and brought Samson's body to be buried next to his father's body. They told how Samson had cried out to God and God had heard and given him back his strength to do this last task. I had to thank God for being so faithful in bringing my son back to Him.

Do you have loved ones who have gone out of God's will? God can bring them back to Him and restore them. He is the only one who can. I just had to believe and pray. Why, I read it in the Holy Bible (they have it up here in heaven, you know!). In Hebrews 11:32-34, it talks about my son. It is written, "Out of weakness we were made strong."

Please learn from my mistakes. Teach your children to desire God's will above their own. And know this promise: God will always hear your prayers and have everything under control. My son had to suffer the consequences for his failures, but God still loved him and took him home to be with Him! Therefore, Sampson, my son, may have seemed cursed but he ended up being used by God. My God can use all things to bring Himself honor and glory! He wants to use you this day!

There was a certain man of Zorah, of the family of the Danites, whose name was Manoah; and his wife was barren and had borne no children. Then the angel of the Lord appeared to the woman and said to her, "Behold now, you are barren and have borne no children but you shall conceive and give birth to a son. Now therefore, be careful not to drink wine or strong drink, nor eat any unclean thing. For behold, you shall conceive and give birth to a son, and no razor shall come upon his head, for the boy shall be a Nazirite to God from the Womb; and he shall begin to deliver Israel from the hands of the Philistines." Then the woman came and told her husband saying, "A man of God came to me, and his appearance was like the appearance of the angel of God, very awesome. And I did not ask him where he came from nor did he tell me his name. But he said to me, "Behold, you shall conceive and give birth to a son, and now you shall not drink wine or strong drink nor eat any unclean thing, for the boy shall be a Nazirite to God from the womb to the of his death." Then Manoah entreated the Lord and said, "O Lord, please let the name of God whom you have sent come to us again that he may teach us what to do for the boy who is to be born. God listened to the voice of Manoah; and the angel of God came again to the woman as she was sitting in the field, but Manoah her husband was not with her. So the woman ran quickly and told her husband, "Behold, the man who came the other day has appeared to me." Then Manoah arose and followed his wife, and when he came to the man he said to him, "Are you the man who spoke to the woman?" And he said, "I am." Manoah said, "Now when your words come to pass, what shall be the boy's mode of life and his vocation?" So the angel of the Lord said to Manoah, "Let the woman pay attention to all that I said. She should not eat anything that comes from the wine nor drink wine or strong drink, nor eat any unclean thing; let her observe all that I commanded." Then Manoah said to the angel of the Lord, "Please let us detain you so that we may prepare a young goat for you." The angel of the Lord said to Manoah, "Though you detain me, I will not eat your food, but if you prepare a burnt offering, then offer it to the Lord." For Manoah did not know that he was the angel of the Lord. Manoah said to the angel of the Lord, "What is your name, so that when your words come to pass, we many honor you?" But the angel of the Lord said to him, "Why do you ask my name, seeing it is wonderful?" So Manoah took the young goat with the grain, offered it on the rock to the Lord, and He performed wonders while Manoah and his wife looked on. For it came about when the flame went up from the altar toward heaven, that the angel of the Lord ascended in the flame of the altar. When Manoah and his wife saw this, they fell on their faces to the ground. Now the angel of the Lord did not appear to Manoah or his wife again. Then Manoah knew that he was the angel of the Lord. So Manoah said to his wife, "We will surely die, for we have seen God." But his wife said to him, "If the Lord had desired to kill us, He would not have accepted a burnt offering and a grain offering from our hands, nor would He have shown us all these things, nor would He have let us hear things like this at this time." Then the woman gave birth to a son and named him Samson; and the child grew up and the Lord blessed him. And the Spirit of the Lord began to stir him in Mahaneh-dan between Zorah and Eshtaol.

Judges 13:2-24

Verse of the Day: Psalm 32:5

I acknowledged my sin to Thee,
And my iniquity I did not hide;
I said, "I will confess my transgressions to the Lord";
And Thou didst forgive the guilt of my sin.

"An Unknown Woman"

There may come a day when you must take a stand for the Lord. Are you ready for this? Your friends and family may call you crazy, but you must stand firm. Your faith may be tested. Can you see yourself passing this time of testing? Here is a lady who, though she is often overlooked, remained faithful to God and to her husband.

I am so pleased to be with you. I am talked about in the Holy Bible at least six times, but my name is never mentioned. You know my family's story very well. My husband was Noah. His name means "rest." Why, I don't know, because he very rarely rested. I'll never forget the day when he came into our home and said, "Wife, I'm going to build an ark. God told me to do so." First, I had to get him to explain to me what an ark was. He was so calm, and I was—well, you know about us women—I was wondering what the neighbors and our families were going to think and how we were going to live. You see, I had forgotten something very important. My husband was very close to God, and he had taught me to worship God also. We were simply to obey God's commands and let Him take care of everything else. So I hugged my husband and tried to be supportive, but the abuse from others was amazing. Why, even my own mother said to me I had married a crazy man and that I should leave him. I learned that sometimes you must shut your family, friends, and the world out and concentrate on serving God and not them.

The relationship between my husband and me became so wonderful! We had learned to trust God. Now our three sons believed in both God and their father and were helping their father build the ark. What a joy to see my family working together to obey God's commands! Think about yourself and your family right now. Are you striving to be obedient to whatever God calls you to do?

Well, back to my story. We'd gone through all of this and God told Noah rain was coming in seven days and we needed to get the animals into the ark. Now I was thinking, "How are we going to do this?!" There I am again, taking my eyes off God. When it was time, you could see animals coming to the ark just as calm as could be, two by two, male and female. God had it all taken care of—amazing!

We all went into the ark—Noah and I, our three sons and their wives, and all those animals! Then, finally, God shut the door. It started to rain and the waters came up. Soon I heard the ark creak and groan. All of a sudden, it started to move (And so did my stomach!). I had never felt anything like this before. There I sat with all these sounds and movements going on around me, and I looked around and there was my family praying and worshipping God amidst the storm. Amazingly, I had perfect peace.

For forty days, it rained. We cared for the animals and each other while waiting to see what God was going to do next. Have you ever just stopped and wondered what God was going to do with you next? Are you prepared to do whatever He asks? We felt the ark make a soft bump and then settle down. The water was receding. At last the day came when Noah opened the door. Our new beginning!

Immediately, my husband built an altar to praise God. God had brought us through the storm! My eyes filled with tears of joy as I watched my family praising God.

My friend, praise God and trust Him completely this day. Then watch without fear as God carries you through the storms of your life.

These are the records of the generations of Noah. Noah was a righteous man, blameless in his time; Noah walked with God. And Noah became the father of three sons: Shem, Ham, and Japheth.
Genesis 6:9 and 10

Then, Noah and his sons and his wife and his sons' wives with him entered the ark because of the water of the flood.
Genesis 7:7

Then God spoke to Noah, saying, "Go out of the ark, you and your wife and your sons and your sons' wives with you."
Genesis 8:15 and 16

So Noah went out, and his sons and his wife and his sons' wives with him. Every beast, every creeping thing, and every bird, everything that moves on the earth, went out by their families from the ark. Then Noah built and altar to the Lord, and took of every clean animal and of every clean bird and offered burnt offerings on the altar.
Genesis 8:18-20

Verse of the Day: Psalm: 5:11

But let all who take refuge in Thee be glad,
Let them ever sing for joy;
And mayest Thou shelter them,
That those who love Thy name may exult in Thee.

"A Committed Woman"

Have you ever wondered just how committed you are to the Lord? Is He really first in all things in your life? Sometimes we need to analyze the answers to these questions. Just think—what motivates your life? Here is a lady who was totally committed to the Lord, and she tells how she was used by the Lord.

My name is Phoebe. I was just a little girl when I heard about the crucifixion of Jesus. When I heard the story, I was very confused as to why we killed a man who had done no crime. I was born in 15 A.D., so the crucifixion and resurrection of Jesus was often talked about. How could someone who was dead become alive again? I had many questions. I heard from people who had actually seen Him after His resurrection. "Should I believe all of this?" I wondered. I was just like any other girl at that time. I wanted a good marriage and several children. My father had arranged a fine marriage for me. I was about sixteen years old. But the young man died. What was I to do? My father and mother were both killed in an accident. I was all alone. It was then that I listened to what people were saying about Jesus. Everything in my life had been taken away from me. I was confused and depressed.

How was I to find a husband now? I had no one to arrange a marriage for me. But as I listened to more about Jesus and how He loved us so much that He died for us, I became at peace. I knew my life had to be about Jesus and serving Him. I worked in a friend's shop and I would talk to the customers about Jesus. Some of them said they were too busy to listen. I warned them that I had been the same way and I had lost everything before I finally listened and accepted Christ. If Jesus wanted me to have a husband, He would bring one to me. But if He wanted me to remain single, I would be content with that, too. I learned to enjoy serving others.

A man named Paul came to our town of Cenchrea. Cenchrea is a port town just about seven miles from Corinth. Paul would come and teach us about Jesus. We had an assembly that would meet regularly. I served the people of our assembly and tried to care for Paul's needs also. This is what gave me great joy and contentment in my life. I knew the purpose of my life was to be committed to serving Jesus and His servants. I wanted everyone to know about Jesus. Paul called me his little sister in the Lord. I had no earthly family, but I had a great heavenly family. Paul had been busy writing letters to other believers. I was surprised yet delighted when Paul came to me and entrusted to me the letter he had written for the Roman church. He wanted me to deliver the letter to them because I was going there to help them learn about caring for each other as they witnessed for Jesus. What an honor! Here I was to carry this precious letter. This was the meaning of my life. It was to serve the Lord Jesus. Jesus had given His life for me. How could I give Him anything less but my life in return?

How much do you really live for the Lord? Is He someone you think about occasionally or is He your reason for living? Give Him your all. You'll be surprised as to what He gives you in return. It is total peace and contentment. People are seeking this in every way imaginable. But it can only be found in Him.

I commend to you our sister Phoebe, who is a servant of the church which is at Cenchrea; that you receive her in the Lord in a manner worthy of the saints, and that you help her in whatever matter she may have need of you; for she herself has also been a helper of many, and of myself as well.

Romans 16:1 and 2

Verses of the Day: Psalm 70:4 and 5

Let all who seek You rejoice and be glad in You;
And let those who love Your salvation say continually,
"Let God be magnified."
But I am afflicted and needy;
Hasten to me, O God!
You are my help and my deliver;
O Lord, do not delay.

"An Enterprising Woman"

Today we find ourselves in the city of Thyatira. It is a city of many businesses and much commerce. In such a city of hustle and bustle, how can anyone stop long enough for religion? Everyone is busy, yet here is where the first European church was started. Here is a lady who can explain how this happened.

I am pleased to tell you my story. My name is Lydia and I was living in Thyatira. My husband was dead and I found myself needing to provide for my family. Now, in my area, there was a certain beautiful purple dye. It was very rare and expensive. It was made by extracting certain oils from a shellfish that lived in a small part of the coast near Thyatira. Because it was so special, Romans made laws concerning who could wear clothing dyed with this color. I joined an artists' guild and became very prominent in the community and very wealthy. I felt very secure. My family and servants were being taken care of and we had many luxuries. I believed in practicing religion. And I always dealt honestly with my customers. The artists' guild I belonged to showed my integrity and business success. Yet somehow I still felt something was missing in my life. I became more religious and attended services and prayer meetings.

One day I attended a prayer meeting with some other women. A man named Paul was there and he started to speak to us. He told us about Jesus and how Jesus had died and then risen from the dead to pay for our sins. We needed to believe and trust in Jesus.

As I listened, it was as if someone lifted the scales from my eyes. Here was what I was missing in my life. I gave my heart and my life to Jesus. This was not getting "religious". This was a "relationship." I was so excited I told everyone in my household, servants and all. They accepted Jesus as their Messiah, too. We were all baptized together, showing everyone around us what had happened in our hearts.

Here I was, thinking I had everything I needed. I was wealthy, had a little religion, and my family was secure. Yet I was lonely, unhappy, and unsatisfied with life. Now my life was suddenly changed by receiving Jesus as my personal Savior. It was so amazing. I didn't know it then, but I know now I was the first European convert of Paul. What an awesome honor!

I invited Paul and his friends to come to my home. I wanted my home to be a place where their needs were met as they went out to preach about Jesus. I kept telling others about what had happened to me and how Jesus had changed my life. Soon we had a church meeting in my home. How special is that?! It was such a privilege to have a church meeting in my home and to help Paul in his journeys. There was times when Paul and his friends could come to my home to rest and get supplies. I could just imagine all the lives that were being changed because of their ministry. There was a time when Paul was put in jail for his teachings. How wonderful it was when he was released and he appeared on my doorstep.

I learned one of my spiritual gifts was hospitality, which means ministering to the needs of others. When I think back on what my life was like before I accepted Jesus as my Messiah and see what my life is like now, I am amazed! My life is full of meaning. Look at your life right now. Have you made Jesus and serving Him top priority in your life?

And on the Sabbath day, we went outside the gate to a riverside, where we were supposing that there would be a place of prayer; and we sat down and began speaking to the women who had assembled. A woman named Lydia, from the city of Thyatira, a seller of purple fabrics, a worshiper of God, was listening; and the Lord opened her heart to respond to the things spoken by Paul. And when she and her household had been baptized, she urged us, saying, "If you have judged me to be faithful to the Lord, come into my house and stay." And she prevailed upon us.

Acts 16:13-15, 40

Verse of the Day: Psalm 51:10

Create in me a clean heart, O God,
And renew a steadfast spirit within me.

"A Persevering Woman"

J ust how important is it for you to be in your place of worship each week? Sometimes I don't believe we place the emphasis on worship that we should. How many blessings do we miss by not being in our place? Listen as a woman tells her story of how she was rewarded for being steadfast in worship.

I so enjoyed going to the synagogue on the Sabbath. Listening to the scrolls being read and watching the sacrifices being made was exciting to me. My family was very religious and our lineage was in direct line to Abraham, the father of our nation. So it was important for me to know my heritage and the faith of my people.

I was about ready to be given away in marriage (at about fifteen years of age) when a strange sickness came upon me. Suddenly, I could not straighten up. Something was wrong with my spine. I was almost bent double. I was taken to many physicians and no one could help. They said it was a curse, but what had I done to deserve this? I was so confused. I knew my only answer was to be found in our God. So I faithfully attended the synagogue every Sabbath. There were many times when I felt pain and just didn't know how I was going to make it, but I did. This went on for eighteen years. I didn't understand, but I knew God wanted me to endure this situation for a reason.

I started to hear about a man named Jesus. Our people had many confusing ideas as to who He really was. Jesus was teaching a new doctrine and healing and performing many miracles. "Who is He?" I wondered. "Is He the Messiah who had been promised to us by the prophets?" I had heard so much about this at the synagogue.

Then one Sabbath I went to the synagogue and there He was. Jesus! Being bent over, I had to turn my head just a certain way to see Him. Then He looked at me. He smiled and called me to come over to Him. I came as quickly as I could. It was so difficult for me to walk. I heard Him say to me, "Woman, you are freed from your sickness." He laid His hands on me. I felt a warmth go through my whole body. Immediately, I stood up straight! I hadn't been able to do this for eighteen years. I knew Jesus was our promised Messiah, and I began to glorify His name. My friends who had helped me all these years were jumping and crying and praising Jesus!

All of a sudden, the synagogue officials began running around and telling everyone to hush. They were so angry. They actually said there were six days to do work and that Jesus shouldn't be performing miracles on the Sabbath! Now I was thinking, "What is their problem? What better day than the Sabbath!" I was delighted to hear the answer Jesus gave. It totally humiliated those synagogue officials.

Jesus said, "You hypocrites; does not each of you on the Sabbath untie his ox or his donkey from the stall and lead him away to water him? And this woman, a daughter of Abraham as she is, whom Satan has bound for eighteen long years, should she not have been released from this bond on the Sabbath day?"

Everyone started yelling and praising Jesus as Messiah. All of us went home laughing and singing and telling everyone we could see about what had happened at the synagogue that day. I was running! Can you believe it? I hadn't been able to do this for eighteen years. What a miracle!

I spent the rest of my life serving my Messiah. There were many times during those years I wondered what would have happened if I had not gone to the synagogue that day. I am so thankful I had been taught the importance of being in my place of worship. How important is it for you? In each of our lives, we will have pain, sorrow, and struggle. I knew the only place to find the answer was to be where God could speak to me. I went and Jesus showed up! The same will happen to you.

And He was teaching in one of the synagogues on the Sabbath. And there was a woman who for eighteen years had had a sickness caused by a spirit; and she was bent double, and could not straighten up at all. When Jesus saw her, He called her over and said to her, "Woman, you are freed from your sickness." And He laid His hand on her; and immediately she was made erect again and began glorifying God. But the synagogue official, indignant because Jesus had healed on the Sabbath, began saying to the crowd in response, "There are six days in which work should be done; so come during them and get healed, and not on the Sabbath day." But the Lord answered him and said, "You hypocrites, does not each of you on the Sabbath untie his ox or his donkey from the stall and lead him away to water him? And this woman, a daughter of Abraham as she is, whom Satan has bound for eighteen years, should not have been released from this bond on the Sabbath day?" As He said this, all His opponents were being humiliated; and the entire crowd was rejoicing over all the glorious things being done by Him.

Luke 13:10-17

Verses of the Day: Psalm 146:1 and 8

Praise the Lord!
Praise the Lord, O my soul!
The Lord opens the eyes of the blind;
The Lord raises up those who are bowed down;
The Lord loves the righteous...

"A Released Woman"

~_ᏩᏍᏎ_~

Actually, the woman today is really a young girl. How can someone so young be in such trouble? Just look at our youth today. So many of the young people are in pain and are struggling, seeking help wherever they can find it. Here is a young lady who found the help she needed.

My parents thought they would be with the intellectual crowd and worship all the new gods. After all, it didn't matter what you believed in just as long as you believed in something, right? We lived in the powerful city of Philippi, and my parents worshipped the god Pytheirs. It was a snake-like god of divination. Being able to tell future events was a desirable trait.

My parents took me to these places of worship and I felt scared and cold. Then one day I felt something possess me. I had no control when it took over my body. What was I to do? My parents didn't care. There were two men there who had heard the spirit inside me tell of future events. They thought it was great and convinced my parents to sell me to them. They took the money and left me to be the slave of these two men. I was so miserable. How had I gotten into this situation? Better yet, how was I to get out of it?! This demon possessed me and my masters made me use its power to tell of future events so they could make money. They would bring people to me and have them ask questions about what to invest in or bet on. My masters were making much money from this demon within me, but I was given barely enough to live on.

Then as I was walking one morning, I passed by two men. They were Paul and Silas, although I didn't know their names at the time. The demon inside me knew them, or I should say it knew who they served. Suddenly, I heard the voice come out of me, shouting, "These men are bond servants of the Most High God who are proclaiming to you the way of salvation!" My mother kept dragging me away to tell fortunes, but the demon kept me going to Paul and Silas and yelling the same words. I wasn't sure why the demon was making me do this except maybe to cause Paul and Silas trouble for teaching an illegal religion. Christianity was not approved by the Roman government. But inside my heart I was thinking that just maybe Paul and Silas could bring me salvation from this demon-possessed life.

I followed this same routine for many days. Then Paul turned and said to the spirit inside me, "I command you to come out of her!" It came out at that very moment. I sagged with relief. I laughed and cried at the same time. My masters were furious because now I was of no use to them. They just kicked me out of the way and left me. They brought Paul and Silas to the magistrate and they were beaten and thrown into prison. Everything happened so fast. What was I to do now?!

Then I felt kind arms around me helping me to stand. She said her name was Lydia and she took me home with her. She told me about Jesus, the name the demon had to obey. Here was the true God. It does matter who you worship. But how could we help Paul and Silas? They were thrown into prison because they helped me. Lydia told me to trust in Jesus and that He had the situation in hand. At around midnight, we felt the earth tremble. I was scared and I ran to Lydia. She just smiled and said not to be afraid. You can imagine my surprise when a couple of days later Paul and Silas walked into Lydia's home. How excited we all were to see them. They told us how the earthquake happened and how the jailer and his entire household were saved. Everything happens for a purpose. I tried to tell Paul and Silas how sorry I was that I had gotten them in trouble. They laughed and said they were pleased I was with Lydia learning about Jesus.

I learned that all things are under God's command. I spent my life serving the true God. You need to look at your life. Who or what are you serving? It may be time for you to give your life to Jesus, the one true God.

It happened that as we were going to the place of prayer, a slave-girl having a spirit of divination met us, who was bringing her masters much profit by fortune telling. Following after Paul and us, she kept crying out, saying, "These men are bond servants of the Most High God, who are proclaiming to you the way of salvation." She continued doing this for many days. But Paul was greatly annoyed, and turned and said to the spirit, "I command you in the name of Jesus Christ to come out of her!" And it came out at that very moment. But when her masters saw that their hope of profit was gone, they seized Paul and Silas and dragged them into the market place before the authorities, and when they had brought them to the chief magistrates, they said, "These men are throwing our city into confusion, being Jews, and are proclaiming customs which it is not lawful for us to accept or to observe, being Romans." The crowd rose up together against them, and the chief magistrates tore their robes off them and proceeded to order them to be beaten with rods. When they had struck them with many blows, they threw them into prison, commanding the jailer to guard them securely; and he, having received such a command, threw them into the inner prison and fastened their feet in the stocks.

Acts 16:16-24

Verses of the Day: Psalm 103:1-5

Bless the Lord, O my soul,
And all that is within me,
Bless His holy name.
Bless the Lord, O my soul,
And forget none of His benefits;
Who pardons all your iniquities,
Who heals all your diseases;
Who redeems your life from the pit,
Who crowns you with loving-kindness and compassion;
Who satisfies your years with good things,
So that your youth is renewed like the eagle.

"A Serving Woman"

⁓୧ଚ⁓

A re you a "nesting" type of person? Do you just like getting settled in and feeling secure about the future? Here is a woman whose life started out that way—but, oh, how it changed. Here is how she met the challenges.

I was just recently married and I lived with my husband, Aquila, in Rome. My name is Priscilla, but sometimes they just call me Prisca. We were tentmakers and had a nice little business. I am of Jewish decent and so is my husband, so we lived in a little Jewish community in Rome. We had started worshipping with a house group that told us about Jesus. He was our Messiah. I was so happy with my home and husband and I felt secure in my future.

Then one day Claudius, the emperor of Rome, made a decree that all Jews had to leave Rome. I was frantic! Where were we to go? We only had a few days to get a few things together and leave town. I had to leave many of my precious possessions behind. My life was so unsettled and I had had it all planned out. Now I was totally confused. Aquila tried to comfort me. I believe this was where our relationship really strengthened. We went to a city called Corinth; it was the capital of Achaia, so it commanded a large trade route. We set up our tent business again and I was getting used to the changes.

One day Aquila came home with a man named Paul. He was so excited! Paul told us so much about Jesus, and he was a tentmaker, too! We asked him to stay with us so we could learn more about Jesus. He stayed with us in Corinth for eighteen months. We had house meetings for believers and Paul preached. What a marvelous time we were having.

I had been married to Aquila for many years, but still I had not had any children. I remember one day I was upset and Aquila sat down with me. He said we must learn to accept whatever the Lord wanted for us and to not let the disappointments in our life take away our joy. I started to cry more, but these were tears of joy. My husband loved me and taught me to love the Lord above all things. We prayed together and gave our lives to the Lord.

About a month later, Aquila came to me and said Paul wanted to go to Ephesus to tell the people about Jesus and he wanted us to go with Paul. Here it was again. I had just gotten everything the way I wanted and now we were going to move again! This was what I needed to do. I knew that, so I packed what I could and we left for Ephesus. We found a place to set up our tent-making business again. Paul worked with us. I worked side by side with Aquila and Paul. Many days we would sit and sew on the tents and talk about Jesus. I enjoyed working with my husband. Our tents were mostly made of prickly, woven goat-hair skins or fabric. The sides had to be sewn together and this took much time. But this was our trade and we tried to do it well. Again, we opened our home for services. It was exciting seeing the faces of the people as we told about Jesus. I was now content with the Lord's decision not to give us children. I realized He had a bigger plan for us and He was giving us His children to disciple.

Why, one day we were at the synagogue in Ephesus and there was a nice young man speaking. His name was Apollos. He had heard a message from John the Baptist and was teaching intently about John the Baptist's message about the coming Messiah. He was correct in what he was saying, but he wasn't continuing on and saying that Jesus was that Messiah. So after he was done, Aquila and I took him home with us and began to give him the rest of the story. He was so amazing and listened carefully. It was like raising a spiritual child. We took great joy in discipling.

After the death of the emperor, Claudius, we returned to Rome. I was getting used to this moving business now. So far I had lived in Rome, then in Corinth, then in Ephesus, and now back in Rome. For someone who had started out wanting to spend their life in one place, I was sure getting around. It was in 49 A.D. that I left Rome, and it was 57 A.D. when I came back. Our friend Paul was preaching and teaching about Jesus. There were times when Aquila and I had to hide Paul from people who were seeking to kill him. It was at those times I would get scared, but then I remembered all of what the Lord had done for me. He gave His life for me to have eternal life in heaven with Him. How could I do any less for Him?

Aquila and I loved each other and loved the Lord. You will see that every time I am mentioned in the Bible, my husband's name is also there. That is because we served together as one. Three of the times my name is first. This is to show we were co-equal in our life and service for the Lord. We would make tents and have churches in our homes. We moved through Asia, Achaeia, and Herakleia, teaching about Jesus as the Messiah. This was a totally different life than what I had planned, yet I wouldn't change anything. I learned that contentment in life didn't consist of possessions and a permanent home. Contentment came when I gave my life to the Lord and was willing to serve Him at whatever the cost. Aquila and I had the pleasure of loving each other and loving the Lord. Then came the day when we were martyred for Jesus. Together we had lived and together we were killed for Jesus. How glorious! We opened our eyes together to see the presence of our Lord and King.

This day let the Lord become first in your life. Let Him lead you into great contentment.

And he found a Jew named Aquila, a native of Pontus, having recently come from Italy with his wife Priscilla, because Claudius had commanded all the Jews to leave Rome. He came to them, and because he was of the same trade, he stayed with them and they were working, for by trade they were tent-makers.

Acts 18:2 and 3

Paul, having remained many days longer, took leave of the brethren and put out to sea for Syria, and with him were Priscilla and Aquila. In Cenchrea he had his hair cut, for he was keeping a vow. They came to Ephesus, and he left them there. Now he himself entered the synagogue and reasoned with the Jews.

Acts 18:18 and 19

Now a Jew named Apollos, an Alexandrian by birth, and eloquent man, came to Ephesus; and he was mighty in the Scriptures. This man had been instructed in the way of the Lord; and being fervent in spirit, he was speaking and teaching accurately the things concerning Jesus, being acquainted only with the baptism of John; and he began to speak out boldly in the synagogue. But when Priscilla and Aquila heard him, they took him aside and explained to him the way of God more accurately.

Acts 18:24-26

Greet Prisca and Aquila, my fellow workers in Jesus Christ, who for my life risked their own necks, to whom not only do I give thanks, but also all the churches of the Gentiles...

Romans 16:3 and 4

The churches of Asia greet you. Aquila and Prisca greet you heartily in the Lord, with the church that is in their house.

1 Corinthians 16:19

Greet Prisca and Aquila, and the household of Onesiphorus...

2 Timothy 4:19

Verses of the Day: Psalm 86:7-10

In the day of my trouble
I shall call upon You,
For You will answer me.
There is no one like You
Among the gods,
O Lord,
Nor are there any works
Like Yours.
All nations, whom You
Have made shall come
And worship before
You, O Lord,
And they shall glorify
Your name.
For You are great and
Do wondrous deeds;
You alone are God.

"A Training Woman"

How important is a good education? We put great emphasis on training our children and we start at an early age. It is a difficult challenge for parents to train their children properly. Listen to this next woman as she describes how she trained her son and how God blessed and helped her.

Hello, my name is Eunice. It means "a happy victory." I am so glad I was named this, for it describes my life. Even when I tried to make a mess of my life, God brought me out to victory. I was raised in a city called Lystra; it was a Roman colony known for its violence. My mother, Lois, was a Jew, but she married a Greek. This was very unusual, but my mother said she wanted to make sure she got married and would have a home. This was not a good reason, but she learned to live with her decision. She only had one child, me. We were very close in our relationship. My mother wanted to keep me informed about my Jewish heritage. So we went to the synagogue and studied with the priests. She made sure we celebrated the Jewish feasts and festivals. My father said he was disgusted with it all, but he let us go. I loved my father and I tried to tell him about our religion, but he didn't want to listen.

One day my father brought home a very handsome Greek solider, and before I knew it, I was married to him. You would think I would have learned through watching my mother go through all of this, but I didn't. There I was in the very same situation as my mother. But we never gave up going to the synagogue and making our sacrifices, as was our Jewish custom.

Then I became pregnant and bore a son. I had a special name picked out for him. I didn't know if my husband would allow it, but he said he didn't care. At last I had a son and I named him Timothy, which means "one who fears God." I wanted to train him in his Jewish heritage, not his Greek heritage. My husband said he must learn both, so I knew this was going to be difficult.

A few years passed, and one day a messenger came to the house. He said both my father and my husband had been killed. So there we were, my mother and I, widows who had little Timothy to raise. We moved into one household and cooked and sewed to make a living. We didn't have many things and you would think we would have been weary and depressed. But, strangely enough, we were happier than we had ever been. We freely went to the synagogue and took Timothy with us. He was such a smart boy and learned quickly. We would go around the house singing our songs of worship to our God and talking about the writings of our forefathers.

One day we were going to the synagogue as usual. Timothy was a young lad now (about thirteen years of age), and we heard a man named Paul talking about how the prophecies had been fulfilled and our Messiah had come, been crucified, and then returned to heaven. What an amazing teaching. We had never heard anything like this before. We wanted to hear more. So for many days we listened and came to believe that what Paul spoke of was true. We became believers. Jesus was our Messiah! We eagerly read the writings and tried to tell others the true message. Paul said to keep studying and spoke much with Timothy. Paul left but said he would return and told us to keep telling the message. Timothy grew up to be a fine young man who worked hard and never neglected the studying of Scriptures.

Then one day Timothy ran into our home and yelled, "Paul is back! Paul is back!" We were so excited to see Paul. Paul was on a missionary journey to tell people about Jesus. That night Timothy came to me and told me he would like to go and help Paul. He knew it would put a financial burden on me and his grandmother, but he felt he was trained for this. I knew in my heart that what he said was true, but it would be so hard to let him go. Through many tears, his grandmother and I got his things together for him to go with Paul. I remembered the day he was born and how I had prayed that God would be with him. This was the answer to that prayer. As I watched Timothy go with Paul, I cried, but I also rejoiced. Who would have thought a Jewish woman married to a Greek man would have a son who went and preached about the Messiah?

God can do great and marvelous things. We need to study His Scriptures and trust His direction.

Paul came also to Derbe and to Lystra. And a disciple was there, named Timothy, the son of a Jewish woman who was a believer, but his father was a Greek, and he was well spoken of by the brethren who were in Lystra and Iconium. Paul wanted this man to go with him; and he took him and circumcised him because of the Jews who were in those parts, for they all knew that his father was a Greek.

Acts 16:1-3

For I am mindful of the sincere faith within you, which first dwelt in your grandmother Lois and your mother Eunice, and I am sure that it is in you as well.

2 Timothy 1:5

You, however, continue in the things you have learned and become convinced of, knowing from whom you have learned them, and that from childhood you have known the sacred writings which are able to give you the wisdom that leads to salvation through faith which is in Christ Jesus.

2 Timothy 3:14 and 15

Verses of the Day: Psalm 103:17-20

But the loving kindness of the Lord is from Everlasting to Everlasting on those who fear Him, and His righteousness to children's children, to those who keep His covenant and remember His Precepts to do them.
The Lord has established His throne in the Heavens,
And His sovereignty rules over all.
Bless the Lord, you His Angels,
Mighty in strength, who
Perform His word,
Obeying the voice of His word!

"An Argumentative Woman"

—⸱ᑖᑐ—

Have you ever found yourself in an argument before you knew it? Isn't it amazing how quickly we find ourselves in disagreement with someone? And usually it is over something unimportant, except we just have to be the one who is right. We seldom take into consideration anyone whom we might be hurting in our quest to be right. Listen as a woman finds herself in that situation.

Yes, I am ashamed to say I found myself in this situation. My name is Euodia, which means "good journey." And my life was truly a journey, most of it good. Let me explain. I am a Jewess and I was a businesswoman in the city of Philippi. Philippi was a prosperous Roman colony in Macedonia. I was doing very well financially and had many friends. Syntyche and Lydia were close friends and, as there wasn't a synagogue, we met by the Gangites River for prayer each week.

One week we went and it changed our lives forever. There was a man named Paul who was there, teaching us that our Messiah had already come. Lydia came to realize this truth first. And soon Syntyche and I listened to what Paul was teaching and accepted Jesus as our Messiah. Lydia invited all of us into her home so Paul could continue to teach us more about Jesus. Can you think back to the first time you heard about Jesus? Just to hear the truth I had a Redeemer was so marvelous! Jesus, Jesus; just to say His name was beautiful. I asked what I could do to show the Lord how grateful I was for forgiveness and a changed life. Paul said to tell others and help others understand the truth. Paul and some others were going to continue on their missionary journey. We tried to give them some supplies and funds to help them on their way. Lydia, Syntyche, and I organized the new believers and would teach them what we had been taught by Paul and help them witness to others. Soon we had a church (a group of people called out to preach about Jesus). We were doing great for about ten years. We helped Paul whenever we could. It was not easy, for there was much opposition and hatred. Of course, this produced some fear, yet we continued on with our task.

Then one day Syntyche and I got into an argument. I got my feelings hurt and I wanted everyone to know about it. I wanted to make myself feel better and make them upset with Syntyche. This was where my "good journey" took a bad turn. You would think that all we had been through together would have made me think about what I was doing. Soon Syntyche was upset and getting other people arguing, too. Just how much do you think was done for Jesus during this time of bickering? Lydia didn't know what to do with us. Word of our bickering got to Paul. He was in prison. It was so embarrassing. Here was Paul in prison for teaching about Jesus and he had to write a letter to tell us to stop the arguing and get back to the business at hand—serving Jesus. How could I have gotten so confused and self-focused that I would forget about Jesus?

Syntyche and I met and cried and prayed together. It didn't matter who was right. What mattered was telling others about Jesus so they could become believers. I had no joy during the time I thought I was right about everything. In his letter, Paul told us to live in harmony in the Lord. We were being such a hindrance to the Lord's work. He reminded us to rejoice and to let our gentle spirit be known to all around us. Has your life journey taken a wrong turn? Maybe there is someone in your life who you need to get together with and make things right between you. Remember to rejoice in the Lord and put Him first in your life.

> I urge Euodia and I urge Syntyche to live in harmony in the Lord. Indeed, true companion, I ask you also to help these women who have shared my struggle in the cause of the gospel, together with Clement also and the rest of my fellow workers, whose names are in the book of life.
>
> Philippians 4:2 and 3

> And on the Sabbath day we went outside the gate to a riverside, where we were supposing that there would be a place of prayer; and we sat down and began speaking to the women who had assembled. A woman named Lydia from the city of Thyatira, a seller of purple fabrics, a worshiper of God, was listening; and the Lord opened her heart to respond to the things spoken by Paul. And when she and her household had been baptized, she urged us, saying, "If you have judged me to be faithful to the Lord, come into my house and stay." And she prevailed upon us.
>
> Acts 16:13-15

Verses of the Day: Philippians 4:4-7

> Rejoice in the Lord always, again I will say rejoice. Let your gentle spirit be known to all men. The Lord is

near. Be anxious for nothing, but in everything by prayer and supplication with thanksgiving let your requests be made known to God. And the peace of God, which surpasses all comprehension, will guard your hearts and your mind in Christ Jesus.

"A Wise Woman"

Do you ever get upset over people fighting all the time? Many times innocent people get hurt. We often hear of people disrespecting our police and officials. They need our help to maintain law and order, not our criticism. Here is a wise woman who understood this principle and saved many lives. Her name is not even given, yet her story is magnificent.

Hello, I am just a woman who lived in a town called Abel Beth-maacah. It was during the time when David was made king of Israel. My town's name means "house of pressure." It was a walled city, so we felt very secure. Isn't life like that? We think we have everything we need and everything under control. We feel secure on our own. Sometimes we just go through the motions of practicing religion. Then all of a sudden, a catastrophe happens and we instantly fall apart and seek help from above.

Let me explain what happened. There I was living my life in my wonderful city. My family and I were doing well. We would hear about the battle going on around us, but we thought we were totally safe. King David was acknowledged as our king and we were good Israelites. What could possibly happen to us?

One day I went to the market and everyone was upset. People were running everywhere not knowing what to do. Someone was yelling for the gates of the city to be closed. An army was headed our way!

"Why?" I kept asking. I could find no answer. It was an army led by Joab, who was from King David. They came to our wall and began to try and destroy it.

People were crying, "They are going to kill us!"

Again, I asked, "Why?" No one would listen or answer me. So, finally, I decided to take matters into my own hands. I went to the wall. Men were trying to put up new defenses and kept pushing me aside. I told them I wanted to ask Joab why they were there and why they were trying to destroy our city. They told me it was useless and to get out of the way. I made my way to the top of the wall and started yelling down to the army below. I shouted that I wanted to speak with Joab. Suddenly, everything got quiet around me. A man came forward.

I asked, "Are you Joab?" He said he was. So I said, "Listen to me." He said he was listening. I think everyone was! I reminded him that our city was considered a city of wisdom and that we were a just city and had settled many disputes. I told him I was very peaceable and faithful to our nation of Israel. Then I got to my mission. I stood up on the wall and shook my finger at him and said, "You are seeking to destroy a city, even a mother of Israel. Why would you swallow up the inheritance of the Lord?" I wish you could have been there! You should have seen his face. He looked like a scolded boy. When I think back on it, I smile.

Joab quickly explained that he didn't want to destroy anything. He was seeking a man named Sheba who wanted to kill King David. Joab said he knew Sheba had taken refuge in our city and he was trying to get into the city to get Sheba.

Joab said to me he would leave the city if we would give Sheba to him. I said I would throw Sheba's head to Joab over the wall. I quickly ran down the wall to talk with the people of my city. They were all excited yet afraid. I explained to them that Sheba was trying to kill our King David. Joab, a commander of King David's army, was instructed to kill Sheba. I told them they would destroy our city and kill many to find Sheba and kill him, but if we gave Sheba's head to Joab, he would leave our city and people unharmed. There were some who said they didn't know if they could trust Joab. I reasoned with them that we didn't want someone in our city who was trying to kill our king. I told them we must do what was expected by our God. So we began searching for Sheba.

"What if we don't find him?" they cried.

I encouraged them to pray to our God and to trust Him to help us find Sheba. "God loves us and will help us to do what is right," I said. I reminded them all of what God had brought us through. Then there was yelling and Sheba was being dragged into the center of the city by some men. The men asked Sheba why he had come to our city and if he held allegiance to King David. He spit and said he wanted to kill King David and said we should join him in destroying King David's reign. The men of the city said Sheba needed to be killed so as not to lead a revolt against our king. Sheba's head was thrown over the wall to Joab. Everyone waited anxiously. Would this be enough? Would Joab honor his word? Soon, we heard a trumpet being blown and we saw the army retreating. I have never heard such cheering and shouting. I was being hugged and kissed. People were saying I was a heroine and had saved the city. All I did was ask a question. You will find many times in your life when you feel as though an army is knocking on your door and trying to destroy you. Instead of getting into a panic, try asking the Lord why it is there. What is the Lord trying to teach you?

111

What is He telling you to do? Simply listen to the Lord and do as He wills. He instructs us in His Word and will take us through the trial to victory.

> Then a wise woman called from the city, "Hear, hear! Please tell Joab, Come here that I may speak with you." So he approached her, and the woman said, Are you Joab?" And he answered. "I am." Then she said to him, "Listen to the words of your maidservant." And he answered, "I am listening." Then she spoke, saying, "Formerly they used to say," They will surely ask advice at Abel, and thus they ended the dispute. "I am of those who are peaceable and faithful in Israel. You are seeking to destroy a city even a mother in Israel. Why would you swallow up the inheritance of the Lord?" And Joab answered and said, "Far be it, far be it from me that I should swallow up or destroy! "Such is not the case. But a man from the hill country of Ephraim, "Sheba the son of Bichri by name, has lifted up his hand against King David. Only hand him over, and I will depart from the city." And the woman said to Joab, "Behold, his head will be thrown over the wall." Then the woman wisely came to all the people. And they cut off the head of Sheba the son of Bichri and threw it to Joab. So he blew the trumpet, and they were dispersed from the city, each to his tent. Joab also returned to the king at Jerusalem.
>
> 2 Samuel 20:16-22

Verses of the Day: Psalm 119:169-175

Let my cry come before
Thee, O Lord;
Give me understanding
According to Thy word

Let my supplication come
Before Thee;
Deliver me according to
Thy word.
Let my lips utter praise,
For Thou dost teach me
Thy statutes.
Let my tongue sing of
Thy word
For all Thy commandments
Are righteousness.
Let Thy hand be ready to
Help me,
For I have chosen Thy precepts.
I long for Thy salvation, O Lord,
And Thy law is my delight.
Let my soul live that it
May praise Thee,
And let Thine ordinances
Help me.

"A Proud Woman"

H ave you ever looked back on your life to see how God has directed your every step? Or, if you are still young in age, have you wondered about where God is going to take you in your lifetime? It is amazing how God leads just one step at a time. Life is full of surprises for us, but nothing is a surprise to the Lord. He is the Master of it all. Sometimes we forget this and get anxious. Listen as a lady from the Old Testament comes and tells about her life of surprises and victory in the Lord.

My name is Elisheba and it means "God is my oath." My father was Amminadab and was of the tribe of Judah, which is of the royal lineage. My name is in two parts. The first, *el*, means "God" and the second, *sheba*, is our word for "seven," which is completeness. My father said that when I was born he gave me this name because he knew God was going to use his little girl in a mighty way. I didn't feel like I was special. We were slaves and worked hard for our masters, the Egyptians.

One day as I was thinking about my name, I realized I loved God but didn't see how I could be of any use to Him. My people were under persecution, but I didn't see any way

115

to help them. Many times I would cry out to the Lord to release us from this bondage, but it seemed as though there was no one listening. Have you ever felt that way? When you are in pain or sorrow or troubling circumstances and you pray but you don't see any results, you think, "Is anyone listening?" I was a young woman and a slave and my circumstances didn't seem to be improving. My faith, at times, was small.

Then one day a man came by with his brother and they were talking about how God had been talking to them and telling them to lead our people out of bondage. Their names were Aaron and Moses. Here was the answer to my prayer. All the time I was anxious and thinking no was listening, God was preparing the way to victory. He was doing it in His timing, not mine.

Then something special happened. I fell in love with Aaron and he with me. Can you imagine that?! I went from a slave to being the wife of Aaron. I thought everything was going to be wonderful. Moses and Aaron led us out of bondage, but many people still complained. Moses and Aaron were continually trying to solve their problems. Do you know I believe sometimes people don't want to be happy and content? They will always look on what is wrong. Anyway, there we were traveling to our Promised Land. Aaron and I were blessed with four sons, Nadab, Abihu, Eleazar, and Ithamar.

One day Moses left us to go up the mountain to talk with God and total chaos happened. Moses had been gone a while and the people began to complain and say Moses was dead and that they were going to die, too, if they didn't build a golden calf and worship it. They said our God "Jehovah" wasn't enough. This was where my husband did wrong in listening to the people instead of God. He let them build this golden calf and let them worship it. Somehow we couldn't remember all of what our God "Jehovah" had done for us.

We felt we needed something else. Isn't that the way it is? We were never satisfied and we didn't want to wait on God. We would rather do something ourselves and that's where the trouble begins.

Moses came down from the mountain and saw what we had done and, oh, was he angry! Let's just say he had a very long conversation with Aaron. Moses had been so angry that he broke the commandments God had given him for the nation. So he had to go back up the mountain to get another set. This time, Aaron ruled faithfully.

My husband had done something wrong and so had I, but we repented and God forgave us. Isn't God wonderful? No golden calf or other god could do this. But God can and He gave us total forgiveness and let us serve Him. God brought the Levitical lineage or the high priesthood out through our children. What a blessing it is to see your children lead others in the worship of the Lord. And everything should now be fine, right? But two of our children decided to do things on their own again. They disobeyed God and offered incense and a strange fire to other gods, which God had told us not to do. Nadab and Abihu died because of this disobedience. Why can we not listen to God? He only wants what is best, yet we think we want to do things our own way. Our other two sons, Eleazar and Ithamar, served faithfully as priests with their father, Aaron.

You can read about our lives and our journey in the Holy Scriptures in the books of Exodus, Leviticus, and Numbers. It was all recorded. It is embarrassing to have your life written out for all to read. People can read about our failures, yet I want you to learn what I have been through so that maybe you can have a faithful life with the Lord...

Life is going to be full of surprises, yet we must be content in knowing our God will lead us through each test and trial. I went from being a slave to the wife of a leader. I had sorrows and fears and I did things wrong, yet my

117

God was with me and forgave me and brought me to the Promised Land. Where are you in your life? What strange and surprising things are happening to you? Trust God! He'll bring you through to victory.

And Aaron married Elisheba, the daughter of Amminadab, the sister of Nahshon, and she bore him Nadab and Abihu, Eleazar and Ithamar.

Exodus 6:23

Verses of the Day: Proverbs 3:5 and 6

Trust in the Lord with all your heart, do not lean on your own understanding. In all your ways acknowledge Him, And He will make your path straight.

"A Fearful Woman"

~~~~~~~~

Now think before you answer this question. What would you do if a high-ranking official told you to do something you knew was against God's commands and if you didn't do it you would be put to death? That would not be a good situation, yet this lady found herself in this position. Here she is to tell her story.

Let's go way back in history when my people, the Israelites, were in bondage in Egypt. This is the time in which I was living. My name is Puah and it means "child-bearing" or "joy of parents." My mother was a midwife. A midwife was a woman who helped other women when they were delivering their babies. It was a wonderful calling and I learned this from my mother and became a midwife myself. I so wanted to have a baby of my own, but no one seemed to want me as their wife. Being an unwed woman at that time was very embarrassing and I felt so ashamed. Yet God had me in a profession where I was made aware of my situation continually. I learned through this that God wants us to trust Him even when we don't understand what situation we are living. I began to praise God and worship Him. I "feared" God, which means I honored and reverenced Him. I simply wanted to do whatever He wanted and I became happy and content. My friend Shiphrah was in the same position as me. Soon we became in charge of all the mid-wives. This was a great responsibility. Then one day we received a summons from the Pharaoh of Egypt. Why would the Pharaoh want to see us? We were just two Israelite women doing our calling. I was really shaking when I walked into the palace. I was in awe of everything around me. Shiphrah and I stood before the Pharaoh and he was ordering us to destroy all male Israelite babies as soon as they were born. I couldn't believe what he was telling us to do! We were dedicated in bringing into the world new life and now the Pharaoh wanted us to kill! I was so scared. I walked out of the palace thinking that I didn't have long to live because I couldn't kill those babies. I looked at Shiphrah and she looked like she was in a panic. We didn't say much as we walked to our home. We were afraid someone would hear us. What were we to do? I said, "You know, if we defy the Pharaoh, he will kill us don't you." Shiphrah said that she understood that this was so. We didn't have much time to talk because we were summoned to go to a home where a Jewish woman was about to give birth. I picked up the birthing stool and we went to the home. Let me explain. A part of our duties as a mid wife was to bring the birth stool. When a woman was about to give birth, she was to sit on a stool that was curved out so that the baby would come down and be born. The mid-wife would cut the cord and then take the baby and cleanse it. Because our water was so dirty, we had many babies who died in early infancy. We learned to rub the babies with oil and salt and this seemed to keep more babies alive. So, let me continue with my story. Shiphrah and I were on our way. Shiphrah asks me, "What will we do if this is a boy?" I said, "Our God is mightier than any ruler, we must obey His commands even if it means death." She looked at me and smiled and said that is what she thought too. We even laughed as we thought how we had spent so much time worrying about not being married yet and now we probably wouldn't be around in this world much longer. We arrived at the home and the baby had just been born. It was a boy. We rejoiced with the family and bathed and wrapped the baby. Through the next few weeks, babies were born and we wrapped each baby boy, we knew the Pharaoh would be learning about what we were doing. And sure enough, a summons came. Shiphrah and I walked to the palace. You talk about being afraid?! With every step, we knew we were walking closer to our death. We stood before Pharaoh and he asks us why we weren't doing what he commanded. We spoke up and said, "You know sir that the Jewish women are not like Egyptian women. The Jewish women seem to be more vigorous and many times have the babies before we arrive. We didn't know if this would save us but we thought we had to try. We held our breath as we saw the Pharaoh thinking. He let us go! He turned away and we could hear him saying, "I'll have to find another way." We walked out of the palace and then ran laughing all the way home. Soon word got out to the people about what we had done. You would have thought we were heroines. All we did was what we thought God wanted us to do. We just wanted to be faithful to Him. Let me tell you, God was more than faithful to us. Not only did He spare our lives but guess what happened next. He brought Jewish men into our lives. We had thought we would never marry. And that's not all. Shiphrah and I became mothers ourselves. We had many babies of our own. What a great God we serve!! God will honor those who bring honor to Him. Think about it. Are you trying to honor God or are you serving yourself? Isn't it time for you to decide whom you will serve?

Then the king of Egypt spoke to the Hebrew midwives, one of whom was named Shiphrah, and the other was named Puah; and he said, "When you are helping the

Hebrew women to give birth and see them upon the birthstool, if it is a son, then you shall put him to death; but if it is a daughter, then she shall live." But the midwives feared God, and did not do as the king of Egypt had commanded them, but let the boys live. So the king of Egypt called for the midwives, and said to them, "Why have you done this thing, and let the boys live? And the midwives said to Pharaoh, "Because the Hebrew women are not as the Egyptian women; for they are vigorous, and they give birth before the midwife can get to them." So God was good to the midwives, and the people multiplied, and became very mighty.

Exodus 1:15-21

Verses of the Day: Psalm 145:18-20

The Lord is near to all who call upon Him
In truth.
He will fulfill the desire of
Those who fear Him;
He will also hear their cry
And will save them.
The Lord keeps all who
Love Him;
But all the wicked, He
Will destroy.

"An Armed Woman"

W hen a crisis occurs, people tend to run and hide and become confused. It is a time when it is hard to concentrate and believe that God is still in control. Sometimes we need to stop and listen to God and let Him show us what to do instead of trying to handle the situation ourselves. This is hard to do. We tend to instantly react. Here is a woman who reacted to a volatile situation.

It is always exciting to tell my story. I lived in a city called Thebez. It is just an ordinary Israelite city. My parents totally believed in our God. Many times they would tell me the stories of how our God had saved our people. Although my parents raised me to live in faith of our God, I would hear many people in the city who worshiped different Gods. I wouldn't understand why they would do this. They knew the same stories I did but they chose to believe in other gods because they said it was more entertaining. They didn't want to live by God's rules. Things were going pretty well and they didn't need a god they said. They didn't want any god telling them what to do. They just wanted a religion that was enjoyable and non-invasive. I and others tried to tell them that they only had all these wonderful things because our God gave it to them. People just wanted to live their own way. I didn't think anything would get their attention. But one day a messenger came to our city and told of how Abimelech and his men had destroyed the city of Shechem, a city close to us. Abimelech wanted to be the ruler of the people of Israel. The people had run to their tower, but Abimelech burned them all. The messenger said that Abimelech and his men were on their way to our city to destroy it. That's when total chaos began. People were running and screaming all through the city. The elders were instructing the people to bury their riches and to arm themselves. "With what?" They said. We didn't have many soldiers as our city was one of craft guilds and the grinding of grain. People didn't seem to be able to think rationally. I tried to tell them that we needed to get together and seek God's answer to the situation. Only a few would listen to me. Who am I? I'm just a woman who worked in the grinding of grain. What could I know? I knew I didn't know, but I knew who could give us the answer if we would just go to Him. I prayed and God gave me a great peace. You see real peace is when you know God has everything taken care of even in the midst of conflicts. Then, all of a sudden, there they were. Abimelech and his men were in the city. The elders yelled for all of the people to run to the tower in the middle of the city. We had some bows and arrows and our people could shoot down at Abimelech and his men. Many of my people were crying and saying that we were all going to die. We ran to the top of the tower. The only thing I knew to do was continue to pray for His direction. He brought to my mind the millstone that I used for grinding grain. It was a heavy stone with a hole in the middle. I picked up the stone. I could hardly lift it. I leaned over the tower and I saw Abimelech down below me. I saw him instructing his men to burn the tower and kill us. All I was armed with was a millstone and the faith of my God. I said a quick prayer and threw the millstone over the tower. I looked over the tower.

I was amazed. The millstone had hit Abimelech directly on the head. I just jumped up and down and started yelling. "See what God had done!" We could hear Abimelech telling his sword bearer to finish him off because he didn't want to be known as a soldier who was killed by a woman. When Abimelech's men saw that he was dead, they fled out of the city. I was being hugged and kissed by everyone. The men picked up the millstone and placed it by the tower in the middle of the city. The people were so grateful and wanted to give me many prizes. I suggested that we have a celebration supper. The people were happy to agree. As the elders came to me to present me with honors, I stood up. I knew that this was against our custom. Women were not to address the people. But God gave me the courage. I told the people I was proud to have been able to help them, but the help didn't come from me but from God. "Instead of giving me the riches use these riches to destroy all the idols to Baal," I said. Let's worship our true God and give honor to Him. The people rose and cheered! Throughout the rest of my lifetime, my city worshipped our God. What was done by me was even mentioned in another scripture. My name was never told. It is not important. Every time I walked by the tower and saw that millstone, I remembered what God had done and how He had used me. How wonderful it makes me feel to be used by God. Please remember that God will always give you direction when everything looks hopeless.

> Then Abimelech went to Thebez, and he camped against Thebez and captured it. But there was a strong tower in the center of the city, and all the men and women with all the leaders of the city fled there and shut themselves in; and they went up on the roof of the tower. So Abimelech came to the tower and fought against it, and approached the entrance of the tower to burn it with fire. But a certain woman threw

an upper millstone on Abimelech's head, crushing his skull. Then he called quickly to the young man, his armor bearer, and said to him, "Draw your sword and kill me, lest it be said of me, a woman slew him." So the young man pierced him through, and he died. And when the men of Israel saw that Abimelech was dead, each departed to his home. Thus God repaid the wickedness of Abimelech, which he had done to his father, in killing his seventy brothers. Also God returned all the wickedness of the men of Shechem on their heads, and the curse of Jotham the son of Jerubbaal came upon them.

Judges 9:50-57, 1 Samuel 11: 21

Verses of the Day Psalm 135:5 and 6

For I know that the Lord
Is great
And that our Lord is
Above all gods.
Whatever the Lord
Pleases, He does
In heaven and in earth, in
The seas and in all deeps.

"A Brave Woman"

_⟨⟩ ⟨⟩_

Do you like to have everything in order and planned out? It gives us security to know what we will be doing and where we will be living in the future. Here is a woman who thought she was going to have a nice, ordinary, uneventful life. But God had an unusual task in store for her.

Hello, my name is Zeruiah, which means "a balm from Jehovah." You see, my father, Jesse, had many sons before I came along. My father said I was a sweet fragrance from God. My father loved God very much and taught us all to honor God. We all grew up in a household that was loving and hardworking. My father had a very nice Jewish young man picked out for me. I thought my life was all set. I felt very protected with seven older brothers and I was considered gentle and shy.

Then one day Samuel came to visit with my father. It was an honor to have him in our home. The women were busy preparing a special meal when, all of a sudden, Jesse, my father, began calling in all of my brothers. "It wasn't time to eat yet so why is this happening?" I thought. Then I heard them call for someone to go and get David. He was my youngest brother who was out keeping our sheep. What was happening? I looked out and saw David running to our home. We all gathered together later as my father explained to us Samuel had anointed David as the next king of our people. You can imagine my amazement. My brother was to be a king! My family had always served King Saul, but Samuel said God had spoken to him that since Saul was serving his own way and not listening to God, it was time for a new king.

My nice, calm life was turned upside down. First, the young man to whom I was promised would not marry me because he didn't agree with David being made king. He didn't think that David was good enough to be king, so I said I didn't want to marry him anyway. Everyone was surprised when I spoke up. Sometimes even though you are gentle and shy, you have to speak up for what is right. If God wanted David to be king, then I was going to believe it was so. It didn't make sense to me, but my God was great and He was always right. I learned to speak out for what was right. I remember my brother David laughing and hugging me after he heard my defending him.

One day my father came to me and said he had found another husband for me. This one loved God and trusted God's servant, Samuel, as knowing the true will of God. He said he would serve David as his king. What a marvelous wedding we had! Now I thought my life was calm again and everything was secure again. My husband and I were blessed with three sons: Abishai, Joab, and Asahel.

Then one day a messenger arrived with the news my husband had been killed in battle. There I was with three young boys to raise. I prayed that God would give me the strength to raise these young boys properly. I tried my best to teach them to love God and be strong.

Being the sister of a king was not easy. People expected me to be forceful and spirited. This was totally against my personality. I learned God would be with me and teach me to be what He wanted.

My three sons and I spent much time with David. Abishai, Joab, and Asahel learned to be great warriors. You will read much about them in the Scriptures. I wanted them to stay at home and get positions out of harm's way. But they felt God's call to be warriors in David's army. It was hard to let them go, but I was proud of them.

Then one day Asahel was brought home to me, killed in battle. As I cried, Abishai and Joab told me how Asahel had not run from his mission and did not turn away either to the right or the left but went straight to do what was right. Just as God had taught us. We took his body to be buried in Bethlehem. Abishai and Joab turned to me and said they must return to serve David. I knew this was right and I watched them go.

My sons are mentioned more than twenty-five times in the Bible and are known as the sons of Zeruiah. I was to be a "balm from Jehovah." I thought I was to simply be an ordinary Jewish woman who served her family. I now realize God wanted my life to be used to bring Him warriors for His kingdom. We need to continue to be warriors in God's kingdom. We need young people who will desire to honor and serve God and not want all the things of this world. We need to help them realize what they do for God is everlasting. I went from an ordinary life only concerned about me to realizing all I had, even my children, was God's and His will was more important than mine.

And Absalom set Amasa over the army on place of Joab. Now Amasa was the son of a man whose name was Ithra the Israelite, who went in to Abigail the daughter of Nahash, sister of Zeruiah, Joab's mother.

2 Samuel 17:25

Now the three sons of Zeruiah were there, Joab and Abishai and Asahel; and Asahel was as swift-footed as one of the gazelles which is in the field.

2 Samuel 2:18

And their sisters were Zeruiah and Abigail. And the three sons of Zeruiah were Abishai, Joab, and Asahel.

1 Chronicles 2:16

Verses of the Day: Psalm 138:7 and 8

Though I walk in the
Midst of trouble,
Thou wilt revive me;
Thou wilt stretch forth
Thy hand against the
Wrath of my enemies,
And thy right hand will
Save me.
The Lord will accomplish
What concerns me;
Thy lovingkindness, O Lord,
Is everlasting;
Do not forsake the works of Thy hands.

"A Betrayed Woman"

Have you ever been in an embarrassing situation where you just wanted to sink into a hole? Sometimes God uses those times to bring us close to Him because we have nowhere else to turn. Listen as a woman tells about her most embarrassing moment and how it changed her life.

My name is never mentioned in the Holy Scriptures, but my story is well-known. Let me begin with what is not told. I lived in the city of Jerusalem. *Jerusalem* means "a place of peace," but I had little peace in my life. It just seemed as though I went from one heartache to another. I came to a place in my life where my family was gone and I didn't have a father to find me a husband. I was on my own without a way of sustaining myself from day to day. What was I to do? I couldn't find a way of earning a living, so I went the way so many have done before me and began to sell myself. I became a prostitute. I know what you're saying—"How could you do that?" But I just didn't care anymore and I didn't feel like anyone else did either.

One morning a man came to me and said he wanted me to come to these rooms he had and to be with him. He offered me an unusually large price and I knew this amount would allow me to have some time before my next encounter. I was surprised because he wanted me in the morning hour; most of my requests were in the evening. But I went to the rooms he told me about that morning. He seemed so nervous. I thought he was afraid because you must know that to be caught in adultery was a sin and we would be stoned to death. I just didn't care. I was dead in all feeling anyway, or so I thought. He told me to disrobe as he roamed around the room. Then the next thing I knew, the room was full of men. These were official men—I mean scribes and Pharisees. We were doomed. Yet they just looked at the man and told him to go and he ran from the room. Why were they letting him go? Our law said that both the man and woman caught in adultery were to be stoned to death.

They threw a robe at me and dragged me out of the rooms. I was pulling and trying my best to get away, but they held on to me. I thought they were taking me to a judge, but they kept dragging me across the city. And there I was at the temple. Why were they bringing me here? As they pulled me into the temple, I saw a man teaching and then they threw me at His feet. I was trembling and totally humiliated. I pulled my robe around me as I could feel all the eyes upon me. I could hear the men telling this man they called Jesus I had been caught in the very act of adultery and that the law of Moses stated I should be stoned. Then I heard them as Jesus said what He thought should be done with me. I couldn't understand why they would be asking him this; didn't they just say I should be stoned? I started thinking, "Why would they want to know what Jesus thought? Who is this Jesus?" He didn't answer them. He just started writing in the dirt next to me. When they kept asking him, He stood up. And then He said the most amazing thing.

He said, "He that is without sin among you, let him first cast a stone at her." Then He stooped down and began to write in the dirt again. I looked up and saw the men leaving one by one. And then there was just Jesus and me. What had just happened?! Then Jesus looked into my eyes. Oh, what a moment!

He said to me, "Woman, where are thine accusers? Hath no man condemned thee?"

As I looked on Him, I knew who He was. He was our promised Messiah. I said, "No man, Lord."

And He said to me, "Neither do I condemn thee, go and sin no more."

Here was the one who could condemn me, the Messiah, yet He said He would not. For the first time in my life, I felt alive! What would I do now? I had no desire to return to the life I once lived. I just wanted to learn more about Jesus. What could I possibly do to show Jesus how thankful I was for this new life? I became a follower of Jesus. I saw that Jesus needed people to see to the day-to-day needs of Himself and His disciples. I could bring water to them or cook their meals or wash their clothes. Maybe these seem like such menial tasks, but I was honored to serve with the others in doing these tasks. While many still knew me as a prostitute, Jesus saw my clean heart. Those of us who followed after Jesus would often talk about how our lives were before we met Him. We were all in agreement that our lives now had meaning and true joy. We didn't know what was going to happen next, but we looked forward to each day.

For a little over three years, I served the Master. Then came the day Jesus was arrested and crucified. I couldn't understand how this could happen. I was there. I stood at the foot of the cross. I remembered the day I was thrown at His feet in total humiliation and how He gave me a new life. Now He was being humiliated with the death on the cross. I deserved my humiliation; He did not. I couldn't imagine my life without Jesus.

After they took Jesus' body to be buried, I went with some of the women with whom I had served Jesus. We started to pray and seek what to do next. Three days later, I went down to the market and began to hear the most astounding things. Some said Jesus' body was missing and some said it had been stolen. I ran back to tell the women and they were saying Jesus had risen from the dead. I couldn't take all of this in, but then a few days later guess who I saw? It was Him! It was Jesus! He had risen from the dead. He had paid the final payment for our sin—my sin. Victory was His and victory is mine!

My life went from total humiliation to total victory. Your life can be the same. You never have to feel that no one cares or that your life is meaningless. Jesus is there, just waiting to give you victory just as He did for me.

And the scribes and the Pharisees brought a woman caught in adultery, and having set her in the midst, they said to Him, "Teacher, this woman has been caught in adultery, in the very act. "Now in the Law Moses commanded us to stone such women; what then do You say?" And they were saying this, testing Him, in order that they might have grounds for accusing Him. But Jesus stooped down, and with His finger wrote on the ground. But when they persisted in asking Him, He straightened up, and said to them, "He who is without sin among you, let him be the first to throw a stone at her." And again He stooped down, and wrote on the ground. And when they heard it, they began to go out one by one, and He was left alone, and the woman, where she had been, in the midst. And straightening up, Jesus said to her, "Woman, where are they? Did no one condemn you?" And she said, "No one, Lord." And Jesus said, "Neither do I condemn you; go your way. From now on sin no more."

John 8:3-11

Verses of the Day: Romans 6:22 and 23

But now having been freed from sin and enslaved to God, you derive your benefit, resulting in sanctification, and the outcome, eternal life. For the wages of sin is death, but the free gift of God is eternal life in Christ Jesus our Lord.

"An Honest Woman"

Each day is a blessed gift from God. But it is like a present; you must open it to enjoy it. You never know what will be inside that package; you only know it was given to you in love. Honestly, you don't always like what is in that package. But you learn to smile and remember who gave you that package. We don't always honestly like the things we go through in life, but we must remember who gave us this life and how much He loves us and knows what is best for us. Here is a woman who honestly thought she was going to enjoy everything in her life and had to learn how to handle the difficulties that came her way.

My husband is Philemon and my name is Apphia. We lived in the city of Colossal and we had a beautiful home with many slaves to serve us. My husband was wonderful; his name means "friendship" and he brought joy and comfort to me and our household. My life was bright and beautiful except for the fact that I couldn't seem to be able to have any children. But my husband was faithful and loving. I met with my physicians, but no one could help. I went to my husband and honestly told him I would not be able to give him an heir and that I was not going to live up to my name, for Apphia means "that which is fruitful." Philemon was so wise and loving and said our God could do all things and that we must look to Him.

A little time later, we met a man named Paul who instructed us into believing the truth our promised Messiah had come. How exciting was this news! There were many converts and we opened up our home as a meeting place.

One day I went to Philemon and I could see he was very upset. When I asked what was wrong, he said one of his best servants, Onesimus, had stolen some valuables and run away. He said he was sad because this meant Onesimus must be put to death if he was ever found. Philemon looked at me and said he was not going to try and find him. We just wanted to concentrate on serving the cause of Christ. Our people needed to have the refreshing of their souls that came when they recognized Jesus as their Messiah. Our people needed honesty in their faith. They were tired of all the false-hoods being told them by the priest and the fact that they were instructed to give money in order for their sins to be forgiven.

Then one day we received a letter from Paul, who was in prison. It was an astonishing letter. Our servant, Onesimus, had met Paul and become a believer. The letter started Paul was sending Onesimus back to us not as a servant, but as a brother in Christ. Going against all of our laws, Philemon and I welcomed Onesimus into our household.

I speak much of my husband because he means so much to me. I saw how he dealt honestly with those around him, and because of his way of living many would stop and listen to what he had to say about the Messiah. I, too, tried to live my life in an honest and loving manner. Sometimes many will listen to what you have to say without you saying a word. Our Lord needs our lives to speak for Him. You must be saying, "Sure, it is easy for you. Look at all you had: money, a secure home, and a loving husband."

Let me continue with what happened next. This is where my package went to me that was unlikable. The more we taught about Jesus, the more we became outcasts. We lost our home and servants. But we continued on doing what we knew was right. Philemon, Onesimus, Archippus, and I went from city to city proclaiming the truth.

One day the four of us were arrested and brought to trial. Our verdict was that we were to be stoned to death. Onesimus looked at us and smiled. This was to have been his sentence for stealing from us and running away. Now he was to be stoned for being a follower of Christ. We nodded and smiled back, yet I was so afraid.

As the four of us stood waiting for the stones, my husband turned to me and said, "My wife, you were concerned about not having produced any earthly heir, yet, my dear, you have done more than that. You have produced heavenly heirs. All those you have brought to Christ are your heavenly children. Rejoice and be comforted in this." I hugged my husband and thanked the Lord even for a time such as this. The stones started coming and I could see my husband fall and then I felt the stones. As I felt the pain, I soon opened my eyes to the glorious smile on my Savior's face. My life on earth was over, but my eternal life with Jesus was just beginning.

You will never know what your life will bring; all you can do is love the Lord your God with all your heart and soul. Be honest to those around you and serve Him with a joyful heart. Your message in life must be His message.

And to Apphia our sister, and to Archippus our fellow soldier, and to the church in your house...

Philemon 1:2

Verses of the Day: Psalm 32:5-7

I acknowledged my sin to
Thee, and my iniquity I did not
hide;
I said, "I will confess my
transgressions to the Lord";
and Thou didst forgive
the guilt of my sin.
Therefore, let everyone
who is godly pray to
Thee in a time when
Thou may be
found;
surely in a flood of great
waters they shall not
reach him.
Thou art my hiding place;
Thou dost preserve
me from trouble;
Thou dost surround me
with songs of deliverance.

"A Praying Woman"

~~~꿍꿎~~~

Have you ever felt God moves too slowly and maybe needs your help? Maybe you think you know the answer to your situation and that you don't need God's help. These thoughts lead to many wrong decisions with lifelong consequences. Listen as a woman explains what happened to her when she got ahead of God.

I just wanted to get my life settled, so I told my family to marry me to anyone who would be guaranteed to have the finances to give me a secure home. I didn't care if he was a Jew or not. Of course, my parents only wanted me to marry a Jew, for that was our nationality. All of the Jewish men were too poor for me and didn't have really secure occupations. They told me to wait on the Lord and that He would send the right man to our town of Lystra. I didn't want to wait or live a life of struggling for existence like my parents, so I found a gentile who was a soldier. This meant he was always being paid and I would have a secure home. My parents relented and married me to him.

Now I knew how important our faith was and I went to the synagogue each week. I thought I could get my husband to convert. I was very mistaken. He wanted nothing to do with my religion. I began to see I had been thinking only of my selfish wants and hadn't bothered to try and understand what God wanted for me. I had made the wrong decision, but there was nothing I could do. I was blessed with a daughter named Eunice. You have read her story earlier. I couldn't seem to be able to have any other children. This made my husband very upset because he wanted a son. Oh, I had a secure home and enough finances to have all the necessary things I wanted, except I felt so lonely. But I had my daughter and I wanted her to know her faith and not make the mistakes I had made. So each week we would go to the synagogue and learn the teachings of our God.

Eunice was becoming a fine young lady and I was looking for a nice Jewish man for her to marry. Then one day my husband came home with a fellow soldier and said Eunice was to marry him.

"No," I cried! "She must marry a Jewish man!"

He replied that since I couldn't produce him a son, he had chosen a son for himself. He ordered me to prepare a wedding supper. Eunice and I prepared the supper. I was in tears. Eunice said she would always be true to her faith. I prayed to my God and asked His forgiveness. My sins were being carried down to my daughter. Had I just been playing with my religion? I wanted people to see how pious I was in that I always attended the synagogue with my daughter. I wanted them to be sympathetic to me in my situation since I was married to a gentile. I hadn't come to the point of putting God first in my life. I had centered everything around me. It wasn't until I saw what was going to happen to my daughter that I really repented of my sin of rebelliousness. There was nothing I could do for my daughter except be there for her and pray for her each day. And oh, how I prayed!

Then came the day when Eunice ran to me and said she was going to have a baby. What a blessed event. We prayed together and asked God to let us be able to break the consequences of my sin. Eunice had a little boy. We asked if we could name him. The men were so excited they said they didn't care, so we named him Timothy, which means "honored of God." Now my prayer life was increased to seek God's will in my grandson's life. What a joy to watch my grandson grow. Eunice and I took him to the synagogue each week. But this time it wasn't for show or sympathy. Now we just wanted to become closer to God and learn of Him.

Eunice couldn't seem to have anymore children. Her husband didn't care, as he had a son and could continue his soldiering. Then came the day when a messenger came to my door. He told me my husband and Eunice's husband had both been killed in battle. So much for the secure finances I thought I had. Now my daughter and I had to think about how we were going to support ourselves and Timothy. Eunice and Timothy moved in with me. We cooked and sewed for others in order to supply our needs. I actually was happier than I had ever been because my life was right with God and I could help my daughter and grandson understand the graciousness of God.

One morning we went to the synagogue as usual, but there was a young man there teaching about how our Messiah had already come. He spoke with great conviction. We invited him to our home so we could learn more. Soon we knew what he spoke was the truth. Jesus was our Messiah and we learned to pray for converts. We started helping others come to this knowledge of truth. Paul needed to leave and continue his journey; he told us to study more and he would return. How wonderful that God sent this good news to us. Timothy studied much about the Messiah. Eunice and I knew God had something special for Timothy. We prayed we would be willing to do anything God wanted.

When Paul returned and saw how much Timothy had learned and how he spoke with the people, he wanted Timothy to go with him and preach the Word. Timothy was all we had and we didn't want to lose him, yet I was so thankful God had chosen my grandson to serve Him. Yes, Timothy was truly "honored of God." Eunice and I wept as we prepared Timothy's things for his departure, yet we smiled, too! Our prayer had been answered. The sin curse had been broken. Even though I had made all those wrong decisions, God still loved me and forgave me when I came to Him.

Eunice came to me and said, "Mother, you have been a true prayer warrior and I believe God does forgive and answer prayer through watching you."

You must see God loves you and only wants what is best for you. Wait on Him! But if you make the wrong decisions, as I did, don't lose hope. We have a gracious and merciful God who will forgive you and give you blessings unconceivable to you if you come to Him in repentance. Just say, "God forgive me." He'll be there.

For I am mindful of the sincere faith within you, which first dwelt in your grandmother Lois, and your mother Eunice, and I am sure that it is in you as well.
2 Timothy 1:5

Verses of the Day: Psalm 145:14-19

The Lord sustains all who fall, and raises up all who are bowed down.
The eyes of all look to Thee, and Thou dost give them their food in due time. Thou dost open Thy hand, and dost satisfy the desire of every living thing. The Lord is righteous in all His ways, and kind in all His deeds.
The Lord is near to all who call upon Him, to all who call upon Him in truth. He will fulfill the desire of those who fear Him;
He will also hear their cry and will save them.

Epilogue

Well, there you are, thirty-one women whose lives were changed by their faith. I tried to present what I believed were their feelings and thoughts while living through their experiences. It was nice to sit and *Have a Chat* with them. Hopefully, we have gained joy, encouragement, and practical instruction for our daily walk with the Lord.

A special thanks goes to my friend, Patsy Rhoades, who tried to make sense of my writing and put the chapters together for me.

Now maybe it's time to sit down and *Have a Chat* with our Lord and see what He has for us to do for Him.